Man, life doesn't get any better than this. Magglio Ordonez was king for a day after hitting his unforgettable walk-off homer in Game 4 of the American League Championship Series.

America's pastime: baseball. Players' pastime: autographing baseballs. Clockwise, from left, Justin Verlander, Vance Wilson, Jeremy Bonderman and Jamie Walker sign baseballs. ERIC SEALS

THE 'ROAR RETURNS' BENCH

EDITOR:
Mark Francescutti

DESIGNERS:
Ryan Ford, Jason Karas, Jesus Maldonado

PHOTO EDITORS:
Diane Weiss, Kathy Kieliszewski

PHOTO IMAGING:
Jessica Trevino

PRODUCTION EDITORS:
Bob Ellis, A.J. Hartley, Stephen Mounteer

SPECIAL COMPILATION AND EDITING:
Matt Cammarata, Brian Coburn, Kirkland Crawford, Martin Dobek, Jon Machota, Kyle O'Neill, Neal Ruhl

COPY EDITORS: Dan Austin, Kevin Bull, Steve Byrne, Terrance Collins, Bill Collison, David Darby, Marisela DelaGarza, Vince Ellis, Matt Fiorito, Janet Graham, Maiya Hayes, Jeff Juterbock, Nancy Laughlin, Tim Marcinkoski, Carlos Monarrez, Al Toby and the Free Press sports staff

COVER DESIGN:
Ryan Ford

COVER PHOTO:
Kirthmon F. Dozier

PROJECT COORDINATOR:
Dave Robinson

SPORTS EDITOR:
Gene Myers

DESIGN DIRECTOR:
Steve Dorsey

SPECIAL THANKS: John Fleming, Rick Nease, Tom Panzenhagen, Craig Porter, Mike Thompson

Detroit Free Press

600 W. Fort St.
Detroit, MI 48226

©2006 by Detroit Free Press. All rights reserved.

Manufactured by Quebecor World Dubuque, USA

OTHER RECENT FREE PRESS SPORTS BOOKS

- The Captain
- Not Till the Fat Lady Sings
- Men at Work
- Razor Sharp
- Fishing Michigan
- Hockey Gods
- Hang 10
- Believe

- Stanleytown
- Ernie Harwell: Life After Baseball
- Ernie Harwell: Stories from My Life in Baseball
- Century of Champions

- Corner to Copa
- The Corner
- State of Glory

 To order any of these titles, go to www.freep.com/bookstore or call 800-245-5082

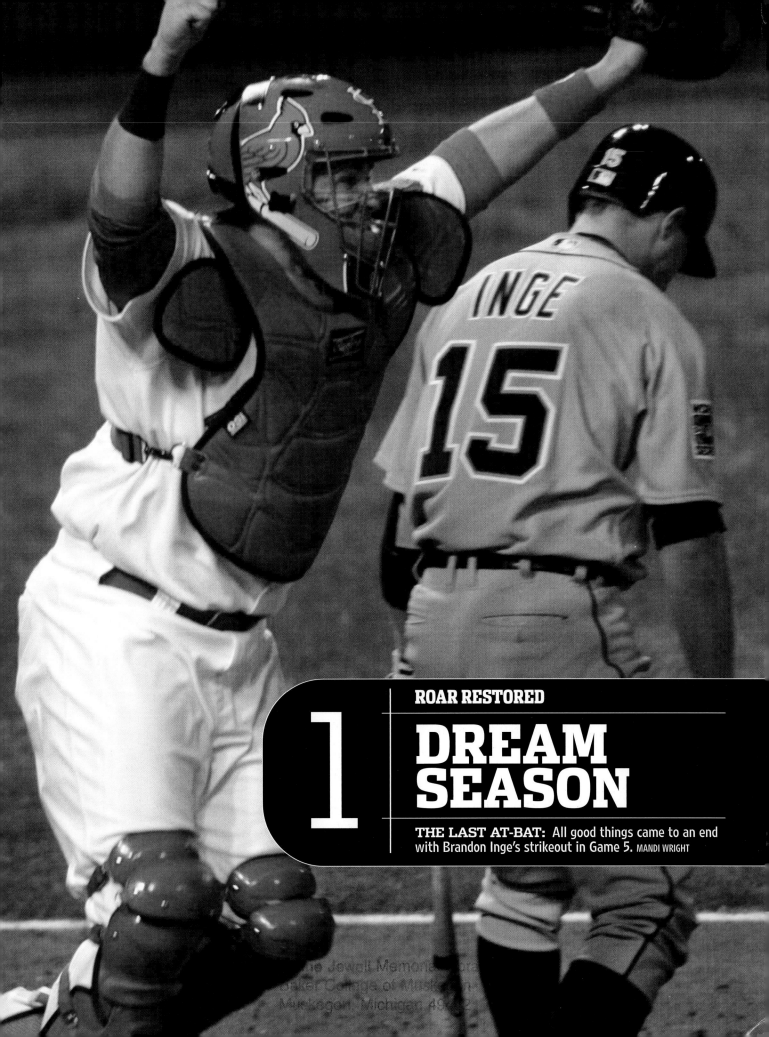

ROAR RESTORED

1 | DREAM SEASON

THE LAST AT-BAT: All good things came to an end with Brandon Inge's strikeout in Game 5. MANDI WRIGHT

Kenny Rogers and Chris Shelton joyfully embrace after the Tigers clinched their first playoff berth since 1987. Kansas City was the victim that fateful day in September.
JULIAN H. GONZALEZ

A great ride

EVEN THOUGH THEY FELL SHORT, THE TIGERS BROUGHT PASSIONATE BASEBALL BACK TO MOTOWN

By Mitch Albom

ST. LOUIS — In the end, they could only watch: watch balls fly past their gloves, watch pitches zip past their bats, watch another team do the infield dance they had dreamed of doing once upon a time, when they were a hot team.

Come in from the rain. A full workweek in St. Louis turned out to be as soggy and depressing as the clouds that never left the Missouri skies. Three games, three losses. A dream deferred. A World Series gone. The Tigers are runners-up, the Cardinals are World Series champions after a 4-2 win in Game 5.

But it was a great ride. Nothing detracts from that. Baseball has risen from the dead in Detroit, and the Tigers have carried our sports hopes from spring to summer and summer to fall, giving us a nightly story and a daily conversation.

"I just hope people realize what this team accomplished coming from 71 wins," manager Jim Leyland said. "And how hard it is just to get to the World Series."

How could they not?

This team gave us kids to talk about — Justin Verlander and Joel Zumaya and Curtis Granderson — they gave us veterans rewriting their history — Todd Jones and Kenny Rogers — they gave us a walk-off home run to win the pennant and 23 shutout innings to make the old men feel like kids again. They gave us the quick, pesky guys like Placido Polanco and Carlos Guillen, and the beefy humor of Sean Casey and the fielding acrobatics of Brandon Inge and Pudge Rodriguez. For the first time in nearly 20 years, they made us remember their names.

What was best was the rekindling of an old feeling we thought we'd lost, like the sensation of riding a bike without holding the handles,

After Game 5 in St. Louis, the Tigers' well-traveled bags head back to Detroit. After this disappointing Series, the Tigers are sure to take a little emotional baggage into next season.

like sledding down a big hill, like giggling with friends in the wee hours down in the basement. Kids stuff. The stuff of our youth — a feeling we had in 1984 or 1968 but figured we would never feel again. Let's face it. The last time any of us enjoyed a World Series, the old were middle-aged, the middle-aged were just out of school, and the just out of school were just out of the womb.

Now we have a baseball team again. The Tigers may not be the world champs, but they are the American League pennant winners, and they are young and full of promise and they are coming back for more next April.

Of course, the World Series will hurt.

The Tigers never seemed to get comfortable on this stage, their footing was unsure, their breathing was erratic, the air seemed different somehow. They didn't hit enough balls safely, and they threw far too many away. If they built a statue to the Tigers' performance in this Fall Classic, they'd have to build two — one of a fielder diving, arm outstretched, and another, a few feet away, of the ball.

It was never funny. But when it starts becoming routine, it's time to go home.

Carded.

"It was a strange series, especially here in St. Louis," said third baseman Brandon Inge in a sub-

dued clubhouse after the Cardinals won the crown. "Weird things happened. Maybe it was the spotlight. It is the biggest stage on the face of the Earth in baseball."

Maybe too big for this young team. Their floodlights went dark with an Inge strikeout just shy of 11:30 p.m. The boys of summer had lost to the men of autumn.

The 95 games the Tigers won in the regular season outshone the 83 of the Cardinals, but that is like comparing high school transcripts to annual reports. When it counted, the Cardinals had the larger bottom line.

"As hard as this is right now," Craig Monroe said, "that taste in your mouth makes you want to come back right away. The off-season is going to go fast."

And should they find themselves next October back on the biggest stage, they will not be the same. The hunger, experience and lessons that they learned will take the field with them, and just as it boosted the Cardinals to the throne, so, too, might it boost the Tigers.

Until that time, the Tigers said goodnight to soggy St. Louis, where if you looked hard enough in the morning, you might have seen a rainbow, and a tired but proud 2006 Tigers team sitting at the end of it, just shy of the pot of gold.

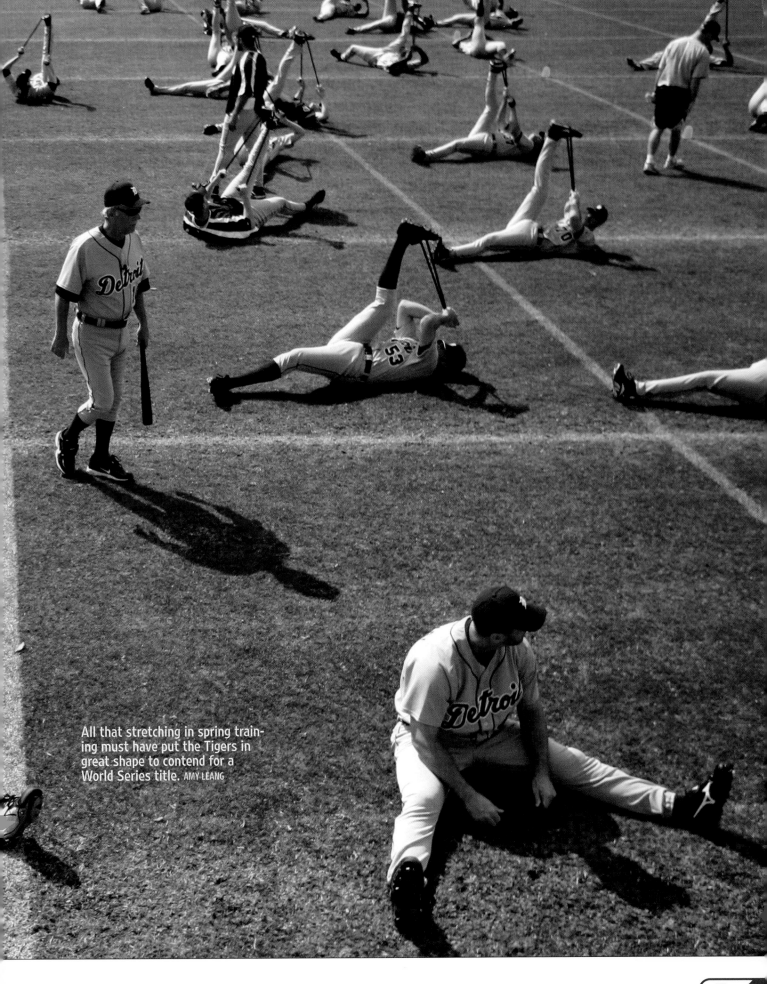

All that stretching in spring training must have put the Tigers in great shape to contend for a World Series title. AMY LEANG

2

THE ROAD TO ROAR

HOME OPENER: On a pretty day at Comerica Park, the Tigers lost to Chicago but showed promise. JULIAN H. GONZALEZ

President and GM Dave Dombrowski helps Jim Leyland put on the Olde English D. "When I talk about people like Tony La Russa and Bobby Cox, that's the type of category Jim Leyland is in," Dombrowski said.

The Ol' Change-up

THE TIGERS MAKE A MOVE IN THE DUGOUT, GOING FROM TRAM TO JIM

ON OCT. 3, 2005 ...

The Tigers axed Alan Trammell with one year left on his four-year contract. Trammell lost 300 games in three years, including 119 in 2003. And his latest team went south for the last six weeks of the season, and his hiring, let's be honest, was more a marketing move than anything else.

Owner Mike Ilitch, a nostalgic type who sensed his baseball team was in danger of a total disconnect from the fans of this city, brought back Trammell and Kirk Gibson and Lance Parrish, and for a few ticket-buying moments, folks thought they were purchasing the spirit of '84. But it was the next century.

"I'm not saying it's a complete necessity," Dombrowski remarked at the news conference when asked about the kind of manager he'd hire next, "but I think experience would be helpful at the major league level at this time."

ON OCT. 4, 2005 ...

Jim Leyland might have issues. Honesty isn't one of them.

In a news conference that was as bizarre as it was refreshing, Leyland managed to tell reporters, "I know very little about your ballclub" and "I don't really know about the American League" and "I'm rusty" and, at his last job, "I stunk."

Leyland, an affable guy who burned out in Colorado, had just got a three-year contract. This is Dombrowski's guy, and the president's tenure now will be judged on how well the man with the white mustache can turn things around.

"Why so fast?" Dombrowski was asked.

"I felt someone else would hire him if we didn't," he said.

Mike Ilitch, the Tigers' owner, did what he does best, reference the Red Wings. "I remember when we hired Scotty Bowman," he said. "One guy can make all the difference."

By Mitch Albom

KEY PLAYER CHANGES

■ The Tigers signed Kenny Rogers (two years, $16 million) and Todd Jones (two years, $11 million).

■ Gone were Rondell White, Carlos Pena, Bobby Higginson, Franklyn German and Jason Johnson.

■ Hello to rookies Justin Verlander and Joel Zumaya, and youngsters Curtis Granderson and Chris Shelton.

HOW THE 2006 TIGERS WERE BUILT

Dave Dombrowski became president in November 2001. He added general manager duties upon firing Randy Smith six games into the 2002 season. All but three Tigers who played on the postseason roster — Omar Infante, Brandon Inge and Fernando Rodney — have arrived under his presidency. When and how each player was acquired:

DRAFT PICKS
▌ 3B Brandon Inge (2nd round, 1998)

▌ OF Curtis Granderson (3rd round, 2002)

▌ P Joel Zumaya (11th round, 2002)

▌ P Justin Verlander (1st round, 2004)

FOREIGN SIGNEES
▌ P Fernando Rodney (November 1997)

▌ IF Omar Infante (April 1999)

MAJOR LEAGUE FREE AGENTS
▌ C Pudge Rodriguez (February 2004, four years, $40 million)

▌ RF Magglio Ordonez (February 2005, five years, $75 million)

▌ P Kenny Rogers (December 2005, two years, $16 million)

▌ P Todd Jones (December 2005, two years, $11 million)

MINOR LEAGUE FREE AGENTS
▌ P Jamie Walker (November 2001)

▌ OF Marcus Thames (December 2003)

▌ P Jason Grilli (February 2005)

▌ IF Ramon Santiago (December 2005)

CLAIMED OFF WAIVERS
▌ OF Craig Monroe (February 2002)

▌ OF Alexis Gomez (October 2004)

TRADES
▌ P Jeremy Bonderman (with Carlos Pena and Franklyn German, from Oakland for Jeff Weaver in three-team trade in July 2002)

▌ P Nate Robertson (with Rob Henkel and Gary Knotts from Florida for Mark Redman and Jerrod Fuell in January 2002)

▌ SS Carlos Guillen (from Seattle for Juan Gonzalez — not THAT one — and Ramon Santiago in January 2004)

▌ C Vance Wilson (from Mets for Anderson Hernandez in January 2005)

▌ 2B Placido Polanco (from Philadelphia for Ugueth Urbina and Ramon Martinez in June 2005)

▌ P Zach Miner (from Atlanta with Roman Colon for Kyle Farnsworth in July 2005)

▌ 1B Sean Casey (from Pittsburgh for Brian Rogers in July 2006)

▌ IF Neifi Perez (from Cubs for Chris Robinson in August 2006)

RULE 5 DRAFT PICKS
▌ P Wil Ledezma (from Boston in 2002)

THE SWEET SIX

Our choices for Dave Dombrowski's top six moves:

NO. 1: Hiring Jim Leyland as manager, Oct. 2005
Dombrowski fired a legend in Alan Trammell and hired Leyland the next day. He found someone who commands the respect a manager needs to control a clubhouse. With an artful approach to handling superstars and role players, Leyland made the Tigers into a cohesive unit.

NO. 2: Trading for Placido Polanco, June 2005
Polanco was a steal from Philadelphia. Not many could trade a reliever for an everyday player, but Dombrowski convinced the Phillies into taking setup man Ugueth Urbina and reserve Ramon Martinez for Polanco, a career .300 hitter. Urbina is now in a Venezuelan prison, where he awaits trial on a charge of attempted murder.

NO. 3: The Drafts, 2002-05
Matt Anderson, Seth Greisinger, Cade Gaspar, Matt Brunson, Mike Drumright. Just mentioning these former first-round picks can make Tigers fans cringe. But Dombrowski drafted young stars Justin Verlander, Joel Zumaya and Curtis Granderson, with Cameron Maybin and Humberto Sanchez waiting in the wings in a rejuvenated farm system.

NO. 4: Trading for Carlos Guillen, Jan. 2004
The Tigers took a chance on an injury-prone shortstop and ended up getting an All-Star for a low price. Dombrowski dealt Ramon Santiago — who later returned — and Juan M. Gonzalez (a minor leaguer who hasn't made it to the majors) for Guillen.

NO. 5: Signing Pudge Rodriguez, Feb. 2004
Before getting a general in the dugout, the Tigers needed a leader on the field. Dombrowski lured Pudge, coming off a World Series season with Florida, with a smart deal that protected the Tigers if the veteran suffered a serious back injury.

NO. 6: Signing Kenny Rogers, Dec. 2005
He was supposed to be past his prime and a clubhouse problem after his assault of a cameraman. But Dombrowski gave him a two-year, $16-million deal. Rogers went on to start the All-Star Game.

IN HINDSIGHT

Some preseason predictions for the Tigers:

▌ **Tony DeMarco, MSNBC.com:** If you're looking for an under-the-radar surprise possibility in the AL, no team has a better set of circumstances working in their favor than the Tigers.

▌ **Sports Network:** The AL Central is a tough division for a young, rebuilding team to be in. Most likely this squad is still a couple of years away.

▌ **Sports Illustrated:** The Tigers bear some resemblance to the 2005 White Sox — an offense with enough balance to make up for a lack of stars, an underrated defense and a pitching staff with a couple of breakout candidates.

▌ **Dayn Perry, FoxSports.com** (picked Tigers second in AL Central and Jim Leyland as AL manager of the year): The Tigers are ... poised (crouched?) to have one of the best offenses in the game.

▌ **Jerry Crasnick, ESPN.com:** Best case: Carlos Guillen, Magglio Ordonez, Pudge Rodriguez and Dmitri Young crush the ball ... Detroit's young pitching is the talk of baseball, and the Tigers jump from 71 to 87 wins.

▌ **The Free Press:** If Leyland's sharp tongue stings the Tigers into a fast start ... If Kenny Rogers pitches like the All-Star he was last season ... If Justin Verlander lives up to the hype anointing him the greatest Tiger fireballer ... The Tigers might have a shot at their first winning season in 13 years ... and the playoffs.

Pudge Rodriguez celebrates his winning, two-run homer with two outs in the ninth on Aug. 5 against Cleveland. It was one of many dramatic home runs this season, but it was one of the moments that made Tigers fans really start believing. ERIC SEALS

A truly irregular season

EVERYTHING YOU WANTED TO KNOW ABOUT THE TIGERS' RETURN TO PROMINENCE (AND MAYBE A FEW THINGS YOU DIDN'T)...

By Kevin Bull and Jon Paul Morosi

It's time to take you through the regular season ... Wait, 162 games? Really? Wow, now that's a lot. OK, then, here's all the high points (and maybe a few of the low ones):

NOW LISTEN UP (APRIL 17)

Manager Jim Leyland wakes up the echoes with a wall-rattling rant after a sluggish 10-2 loss to the Indians. "We stunk," Leyland says. "Period. Stunk. And it's not good enough. It's been going on here before, and it's not going to happen." The Tigers fall back to .500 the next day, but never drop further. Some point to that postgame address as the moment when the Tigers' collective attitude changed for the better.

SHELTON'S RISE AND FALL (APRIL)

Chris Shelton sets the baseball world on fire, hitting .471 with nine home runs in his first 13 games. Halfway through April, he is on pace to hit 108. Shelton becomes a media star. The Free Press nicknames him Red Bull. Then the slump. He hits one home run in May and July and bats .205 in June. The Tigers demote him to Triple-A Toledo when they trade for Sean Casey on July 31. Shelton returns in September but does not make the postseason roster.

UNLIKELY HERO (MAY 17)

Backup catcher Vance Wilson homers off Twins left-hander Johan Santana in the Tigers' 2-0 win. Justin Verlander (the probable AL rookie of the year) out-pitches Santana (the probable AL Cy Young winner). The Tigers win the next night, too, and take sole possession of first place.

IN GRAND FASHION (MAY 20)

Curtis Granderson saves the Tigers in the ninth as Detroit beats Cincinnati, 7-6, in 10 innings. Before the first sellout crowd since the home opener, the energetic Granderson pops a two-out, opposite-field home run to force extra innings. The Tigers win after an error on a Craig Monroe grounder. The victory establishes a trend of late-inning resiliency, as Granderson saves roommate Joel Zumaya, who had allowed a grand slam by Ken Griffey Jr., from a loss.

MAROTH MISSES OUT (MAY 25)

Mike Maroth enters the day with the best ERA among Tigers starters, but suffers an elbow injury. He undergoes surgery to remove bone chips and misses three-plus months and does not make the postseason roster.

MILLER TIME (JUNE 6)

The Tigers draft Andrew Miller, the consensus top talent and a 6-foot-6, 210-pound University of North Carolina left-hander with the No. 6 selection. Miller makes his debut Aug. 30 at Yankee Stadium, pitching one scoreless inning.

OH, BABY! (JUNE 10)

Todd Jones sleeps "like a baby," then saves a 5-3 victory in Toronto. Jones had drawn the ire of fans with a horrific stretch (0-3, 27.00 ERA in four appearances) that included a blown save the day before. He did not fall asleep until 4:30 the next morning. Hours later, he gets the win. Afterward, Jones says, when asked how well he had rested the night before: "Slept like a baby. I woke up every two hours, crying." Jones goes on to save 21 of his next 22 games.

KENNY'S 200TH (JUNE 18)

The Tigers' bats propel Kenny Rogers to his 200th career win — over the Cubs at Wrigley Field. The Tigers hit eight homers, tying the club record, in a 12-3 victory. After the game, teammates give Rogers a champagne toast in the clubhouse.

ROCKET DOWN (JUNE 27)

Roger Clemens leaves to a warm ovation at Comerica Park and takes the loss in a 4-0 Tigers triumph. Clemens' final appearance in Detroit — we think — draws a Tuesday night sellout, the first on a weekday since the home opener. Says Clemens: "It's fun to see great crowds here again."

ALL-STAR CELEBRATION (JULY 11)

Rogers and Pudge Rodriguez become the Tigers' first starting battery in an All-Star Game since Denny McLain and Bill Freehan in 1966. Rightfielder Magglio Ordonez also makes the team as an injury replacement for Boston's Manny Ramirez. The AL wins, 3-2, giving the Tigers home-field advantage in the World Series.

THE HOME-PLATE BUMP (JULY 19)

The Tigers-White Sox rivalry reaches a boiling point after Craig Monroe's grand slam lifts Detroit to a 5-2 victory. Monroe appears to

ERIC SEALS

DH Matt Stairs, who didn't make the postseason roster, waits to bat under the lights at Comerica Park in September.

bump catcher A.J. Pierzynski as he crossed the plate. Monroe claims Pierzynski threw an elbow. Pierzynski, punched by Cubs catcher Michael Barrett after a home-plate collision in May, denies hitting Monroe.

JULIAN H. GONZALEZ

After Craig Monroe hit a grand slam against Chicago, he appeared to bump catcher A.J. Pierzynski. Tempers flared as the White Sox and Tigers became a big rivalry.

TEMPLE OF METRODOOM (JULY 30)

Jeremy Bonderman balks in a run in what he calls "the worst inning of my life," as the Tigers lose, 6-4, at Minnesota. In the span of one inning, Bonderman loses a one-hit shutout — and the game. Bonderman goes 0-4 with a 5.50 ERA in nine starts. Over that same period, the Tigers go 17-26 and lose 7½ games in the standings.

TRADE DEADLINE (JULY 31)

The Tigers pass on trading for Alfonso Soriano, Bobby Abreu and Greg Maddux, instead acquiring first baseman Sean Casey. With the Tigers, Casey hits .245 with five homers and 30 RBIs — mostly from the coveted No. 3 spot — in 53 regular-season games and provides steady defense.

A 10-GAME LEAD (AUG. 7)

Two days after Pudge Rodriguez's walk-off homer against Cleveland, the Tigers knock Twins left-hander Francisco Liriano, the league ERA lead-

It's champagne wishes and World Series dreams. The Tigers celebrate their first playoff berth since 1987.

er, out of the game after the fourth in a 9-3 victory and take a season-high, 10-game lead in the AL Central over the White Sox. The victory pushes the Tigers 40 games over .500 at 76-36. "The way we're playing, I don't think — on my behalf — that anybody can get us, if we continue doing what we've been doing," reliever Joel Zumaya says. Of course, the Twins do catch the Tigers, but it doesn't matter.

YANKING ONE OUT (AUG. 30)

With his mother, Marilyn Monroe, watching, Craig Monroe homers with two out in the ninth to beat the Yankees, 5-3. "If I was to pick one game — and I don't like to do this — the biggest game of the year, probably, was Craig Monroe's home run at Yankee Stadium," manager Jim

Leyland says. The Tigers had lost five of their previous six games. They needed a win. Badly.

DMITRI'S DEMISE (SEPT. 6)

Designated hitter Dmitri Young is released amid concerns about his declining performance and detached clubhouse demeanor. He missed much of the season's first half because of a right quadriceps strain and a lengthy stint in a substance-abuse treatment facility.

HOT PLAY AT HOT CORNER (SEPT. 20)

Brandon Inge stabs Joe Crede's line drive, turns it into a double play and halts the defending champions, for good, in a 6-2 win. There were two runners on — and no one out — in a scoreless, series-deciding game between the champion (White Sox) and challenger (Tigers). The

White Sox falter after that game down the stretch.

THE CLINCHER (SEPT. 24)

The Tigers finally mix champagne and sweat following an 11-4 victory at Kansas City to clinch a playoff spot for the first time in 19 years. Andrew Miller strikes out shortstop Angel Sanchez for the final out. "One-hundred-nineteen to a playoff," says pitcher Jeremy Bonderman, referencing the number of games the team lost in 2003. "Unbelievable."

THE COLLAPSE (OCT. 1)

The Tigers lose their final five games, and the Twins catch them for the Central Division title. The Tigers enter the playoffs as the wild card on the road vs. the Yankees, instead of having home-field advantage against the A's. As it turns out, the Tigers would beat both in the playoffs.

Around the league

A LOOK AT WHAT ELSE HAPPENED IN THE MAJORS WHILE THE TIGERS STORMED TO THE POSTSEASON

CAN'T BUY ME LOVE

A $25-million-a-year contract might buy a lot for Yankees 3B Alex Rodriguez, but it won't get him any relief. He had a down season, well, down for him (.290, 35 home runs and 121 RBIs) and was constantly booed by fans at Yankee Stadium. Even his teammates, including steroid user Jason Giambi, and manager Joe Torre criticized him in a Sports Illustrated article for his lack of clutch hits. A-Rod also struggled in the playoffs, and Torre dropped him to eighth in the order against the Tigers.

MUCH ADO ...

It was overhyped as one of the most important trade deadlines in the history of sports. All eyes were on Washington star Alfonso Soriano. He would be a free agent after the season, and the out-of-contention Nationals looked to deal him. ESPN covered Soriano's every move, speculating he might end up with numerous teams, including the Tigers. One report had the rival White Sox making a play for Soriano to prevent the Tigers from getting him. Washington wanted the Tigers' top draft pick in 2005, outfielder Cameron Maybin. GM Dave Dombrowski wouldn't budge, and Soriano stayed with the Nationals.

NO-NO!

Another rookie gave baseball its first no-hitter in more than two years when Florida's Anibal Sanchez no-hit Arizona on Sept. 6.

USE WORDS, NOT VIOLENCE

Devil Rays prospect Delmon

AMY LEANG

YOUNG GUNS

This was the year of the rookie pitcher. Not since Mark Fidrych of the Tigers graced the mound with his ostrich-like demeanor has there been such a buzz around fresh talent. Besides the Tigers' Justin Verlander, above, and Joel Zumaya, Jonathan Papelbon excited Red Sox faithful with his 10-save, 0.00-ERA April. Minnesota's Francisco Liriano probably was the best pitcher in baseball (12-2, 1.94 ERA through July 23) before two stints on the disabled list ended his run. Jered Weaver, brother of ex-Tiger Jeff, pitched so well (9-0, 1.95 through Aug. 18) that the Angels traded the older Weaver to the Cardinals.

Young, Dmitri's brother played well when he was called up for the final 31 games of the season (.317, three HRs, 10 RBIs). But he had to sit out 50 games earlier for chucking his bat at a minor league umpire over a third strike.

BONDS WATCH '06

Barry Bonds' soap opera marched along. Two San Francisco Chronicle reporters wrote "Game of Shadows," a book about BALCO, a California sports nutrition center, and Bonds' involvement with it. The writers were sentenced to jail time for not divulging the sources who leaked federal grand jury testimony linking Bonds and other athletes to BALCO and taking performance-enhancing supplements. During the BALCO controversy, Bonds passed Babe Ruth for No. 2 on the all-time home run list May 28 with his 715th homer. After a 26-home run season, Bonds, a free agent, stands 21 behind Hank Aaron's record of 755.

HELLO

In an overdue celebration, baseball's Hall of Fame opened its doors to representatives from the Negro leagues, inducting 12 players, including former Detroit

YEAR-END TOTALS

AMERICAN LEAGUE

East	W	L	Pct	GB	Home	Road
y-New York	97	65	.599	—	50-31	47-34
Toronto	87	75	.537	10.0	50-31	37-44
Boston	86	76	.531	11.0	48-33	38-43
Baltimore	70	92	.432	27.0	40-41	30-51
Tampa Bay	61	101	.377	36.0	41-40	20-61

Central	W	L	Pct	GB	Home	Road
y-Minnesota	96	66	.593	—	54-27	42-39
x-Detroit	95	67	.586	1.0	46-35	49-32
Chicago	90	72	.556	6.0	49-32	41-40
Cleveland	78	84	.481	18.0	44-37	34-47
Kansas City	62	100	.383	34.0	34-47	28-53

West	W	L	Pct	GB	Home	Road
y-Oakland	93	69	.574	—	49-32	44-37
Los Angeles	89	73	.549	4.0	45-36	44-37
Texas	80	82	.494	13.0	39-42	41-40
Seattle	78	84	.481	15.0	44-37	34-47

NATIONAL LEAGUE

East	W	L	Pct	GB	Home	Road
y-New York	97	65	.599	—	50-31	47-34
Philadelphia	85	77	.525	12.0	41-40	44-37
Atlanta	79	83	.488	18.0	40-41	39-42
Florida	78	84	.481	19.0	42-39	36-45
Washington	71	91	.438	26.0	41-40	30-51

Central	W	L	Pct	GB	Home	Road
y-St. Louis	83	78	.516	—	49-31	34-47
Houston	82	80	.506	1.5	44-37	38-43
Cincinnati	80	82	.494	3.5	42-39	38-43
Milwaukee	75	87	.463	8.5	48-33	27-54
Pittsburgh	67	95	.414	16.5	43-38	24-57
Chicago	66	96	.407	17.5	36-45	30-51

West	W	L	Pct	GB	Home	Road
y-San Diego	88	74	.543	—	43-38	45-36
x-Los Angeles	88	74	.543	—	49-32	39-42
San Francisco	76	85	.472	11.5	43-38	33-47
Arizona	76	86	.469	12.0	39-42	37-44
Colorado	76	86	.469	12.0	44-37	32-49

x-Wild card; y-division champ

Stars standout Andy (Lefty) Cooper. Reliever Bruce Sutter also joined.

GOOD-BYE

Just days after his Yankees lost in the American League Division Series to the Tigers, pitcher Cory Lidle, 34, died when his plane crashed into a building on Manhattan's upper East Side.

COMPILED BY KYLE O'NEILL

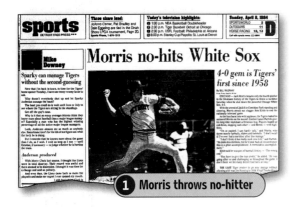

1 Morris throws no-hitter

2 Tigers win home opener

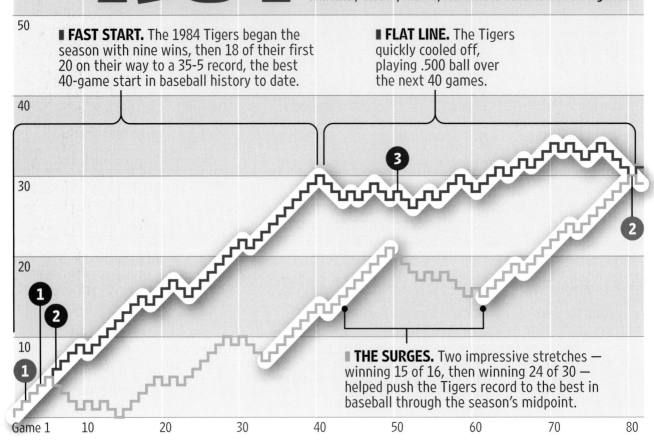

60 games above .500

1984

THE 1984 "BLESS YOU BOYS" TIGERS streaked to a 35-5 start, shook off the Toronto Blue Jays for the division title and beat the San Diego Padres in the World Series. Parrish, Trammell, Whitaker, Gibson, Morris, Hernandez became Detroit legends.

■ **FAST START.** The 1984 Tigers began the season with nine wins, then 18 of their first 20 on their way to a 35-5 record, the best 40-game start in baseball history to date.

■ **FLAT LINE.** The Tigers quickly cooled off, playing .500 ball over the next 40 games.

■ **THE SURGES.** Two impressive stretches — winning 15 of 16, then winning 24 of 30 — helped push the Tigers record to the best in baseball through the season's midpoint.

Game 1   10   20   30   40   50   60   70   80

1 Tigers blast Royals

2 '06 Tigers match '84 team

Mike Downey

Tigers and fans are happy; why's front office grouchy?

Tigers fly past Jays in 10th inning, 6-3

③ **Detroit beats Toronto in extra innings**

sports

Bergman homer beats Jays

George Puscas
Love letters

Would Michigan Tigers feel at home in Detroit?

④ **Tigers sweep Jays in late-season series**

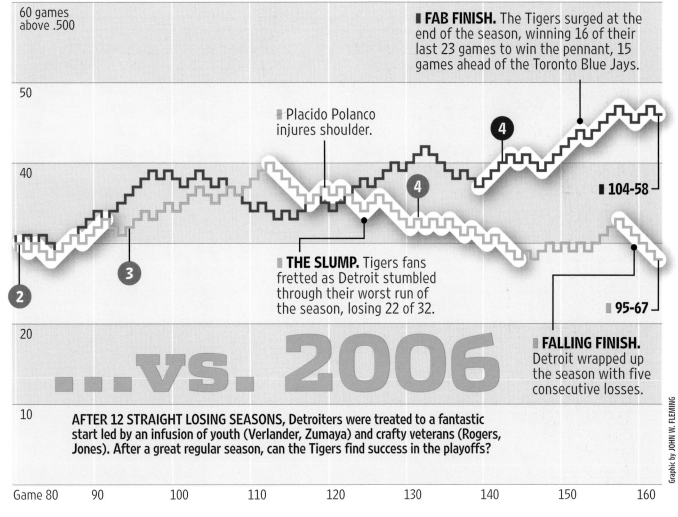

60 games above .500

50

40

20

10

■ **FAB FINISH.** The Tigers surged at the end of the season, winning 16 of their last 23 games to win the pennant, 15 games ahead of the Toronto Blue Jays.

■ Placido Polanco injures shoulder.

④

④

■ 104-58

■ **THE SLUMP.** Tigers fans fretted as Detroit stumbled through their worst run of the season, losing 22 of 32.

■ 95-67

■ **FALLING FINISH.** Detroit wrapped up the season with five consecutive losses.

...vs. 2006

AFTER 12 STRAIGHT LOSING SEASONS, Detroiters were treated to a fantastic start led by an infusion of youth (Verlander, Zumaya) and crafty veterans (Rogers, Jones). After a great regular season, can the Tigers find success in the playoffs?

Game 80   90   100   110   120   130   140   150   160

② ③

Graphic by JOHN W. FLEMING

Ain't it grand?

Monroe's slam finally gives Tigers clout against Sox; Bonderman solid

③ **Monroe slam beats Chisox**

SPORTS

DETROIT 7, CLEVELAND 1

WINNERS AT LAST

Non-losing season first for Tigers since 1993 | Rogers plays stopper as 4-game losing streak ends

Williams waiting to play

④ **Tigers assured of winning season**

3 | THE TEAM

THE WIZARD: The Tigers credited their success to Jim Leyland, their gray-haired skipper. JULIAN H. GONZALEZ

Win one for the skipper

A RARITY IN PRO SPORTS: TIGERS LOVE THEIR MANAGER, JIM LEYLAND

By Mitch Albom

As his team danced around the field in raucous celebration after beating the Yankees in the American League Division Series, manager Jim Leyland found his wife and kids and kissed them through the backstop fencing. Then a fan raced forward and puckered up, and Leyland hesitated, embarrassed, and then — why not? — he kissed the fan's cap. Champagne was spraying, flashbulbs were exploding, the stadium was thundering and suddenly Leyland was on the shoulders of his players, carried off like a sultan, the kind of ride you never forget.

A year earlier, he made a different ride. A car ride, alone, from Pittsburgh to Detroit. He was taking a new job, managing a team that had become a sad, pathetic story, a real head-shaker, the kind of story that in some ways the craggy, white-haired Leyland had become. After flaming out in Colorado and leaving $4 million on the table, he had not seen a dugout in six years. Then he told his new employers: I have the fire again. If you believe me, hire me. If not, don't.

They hired him. During his news conference, Leyland, who can put himself down in a league with Rodney Dangerfield, tried to be painfully honest. He said he was "rusty." He said he needed to "sharpen up on the game." Asked about the roster, he said:

"I know very little about your ballclub."

AMY LEANG

Leyland rose from fringe catcher in the Tigers' organization to championship manager. He took the Pirates to within a few outs of the World Series. He won the Series with the Florida Marlins in 1997.

Huh? A manager doesn't know the players? Isn't that like a pilot who doesn't know the plane? A CEO who doesn't know the product line?

"I made an ass of myself in that press conference," Leyland later said. "What I meant was I didn't know what made the players tick. I knew who they were. I'd seen them play some ... but you have to find out what makes each guy tick, and I didn't know anything about that."

He does now. He knows their ticks and their tocks. He knows their talents. He knows their

LIFTING LEYLAND: The Tigers carry manager Jim Leyland off the field at Comerica Park after beating the New York Yankees in the first round of the playoffs. The Tigers hadn't won a playoff series since 1984. MANDI WRIGHT

ANNIE O'NEILL/Special to the Free Press

Katie Leyland, flanked by son Patrick, 15, and daughter Kellie, 13, takes a call at the Leyland home in Pittsburgh.

hearts. We witnessed something rare in sports, here, folks. In one season, Leyland, 61, has so ingratiated himself to his players that they tried to win this thing for him as well as themselves.

This is Mike Ilitch's payroll. This is Dave Dombrowski's roster.

But this is Jim Leyland's team.

Player after player speaks about Leyland's influence, his leadership, his wisdom, his confidence. It is not uncommon to hear Tigers players say, "Skip is the reason we're here."

But it is uncommon.

Think about it.

Players today play for themselves, almost never for the coach or manager. Oh, sure, if they win a championship, they might douse the guy with Gatorade or throw him a compliment at a news conference. But to go through a wall for him? To respect his decisions when he takes the ball from them, or platoons them, or benches them? Where do you see that in sports anymore? Maybe college? Maybe.

We have seen Leyland happy, and so have his players, and it is a sight they want to fight to see again. How many skippers can say that? Not many.

JIM LEYLAND

MANAGER **Age:** 61 **Born:** Toledo, grew up in Perrysburg, Ohio.

As a player: Spent parts of seven seasons as a minor-league catcher for the Tigers.

NOTABLE

Coaching career: Spent 11 seasons in minors with the Tigers. Tony La Russa's third-base coach with White Sox for four years. Hired by Pittsburgh in 1986. Won three NL East titles with Pirates, 1990-92; won World Series with Marlins, 1997.

The man: Considered by some a genius at dealing with people, Leyland tends to stars and role players with equivalent ease. When you enter his office — a simple place, no trophies, no celebratory magazine posters of himself, no shrines to his accomplishments — you enter a no-nonsense room dusted in honest emotion. After a game, Leyland often addresses the media while smoking a Marlboro, with his stocking feet propped on his desk. Sometimes, he asks the questions. He is the Tigers' most charismatic skipper since Sparky Anderson.

BASEBALL'S BEST SKIPPERS

Our top 5 managers:

■ **No. 1: Bobby Cox.** Forget the choke jobs in the playoffs — he led the Braves (loaded with talent or not) to 14 straight division titles. He's also a players' favorite.

■ **No. 2: Jim Leyland.** Any memories from a horrible stint in Colorado should be erased. He has done more with less than any manager on the list. Our only beef with him: Forget Big League Chew. He needs to get some nicotine gum.

■ **No. 3: Tony La Russa.** Ranked third all-time in career wins and considered one of baseball's top strategists. But many expected his teams to win multiple World Series (he had just one like Cox and buddy Leyland entering 2006). And his defense of Mark McGwire has been criticized.

■ **No. 4: Joe Torre.** Yes, his four championships were bought with high payrolls, and we don't like spoiled Yankees. But he's had to put up with all those egos — and we're not talking about just the gigantic one in the front office.

■ **No. 5: Ozzie Guillen.** He swears; he makes comments even after his foot is in his mouth. But he has a ring. His players respond to him, and he's one of the few managers who will stay with the pitcher he started deep into games.

KIRTHMON F. DOZIER

Leyland has nicknames for his players and staff, and often mixes them up a bit with profanity. You might hear him say: "What's up, numb nuts?" Or something saltier.

DETROIT'S MOST BELOVED COACH?

Jim Leyland's success follows four other impressive coaches since 1989. And he might be the most beloved of the lot.

Bill Laimbeer: Shock titles in '03 and '06. Carried rep as whiner from playing days to the coaching box.

Larry Brown: Pistons title in 2004. The drama was always about Larry, not his stars.

Scotty Bowman: Red Wings titles in '97, '98, '02. He intimidated players more than inspired them.

Chuck Daly: Pistons titles in 1989 and 1990. Acclaimed as the master of leaving his players alone.

OUR FAVORITE SMOKERS

Jim Leyland said he would try to quit smoking this season. "I'm not saying I will," he told the St. Louis Post-Dispatch in the spring. "But I was reducing until the other day when we walked five in the second inning at Winter Haven. I told the clubhouse kid, 'Go over to 7-Eleven and buy me a carton.'"

Leyland never quit, so, in honor of Leyland, some famous smokers:

■ Selma and Patty from "The Simpsons"

■ Smoking man from "The X-Files"

■ Jeff Smoker

■ Smokey the Bear (Only you can prevent forest fires)

■ Wayne Fontes

■ Scott Mitchell (impersonating Wayne Fontes)

■ Smokin' Joe Frazier

■ Popeye

■ Darko Milicic, the human victory cigar

■ Humphrey Bogart

■ Jerry Garcia

■ Earl Weaver

■ Sherlock Holmes

■ Edward R. Murrow

■ The Tigers (Or was their smokin' hot play-off run just our imagination?)

Kenny Rogers was booed at the All-Star Game at Comerica Park in 2005. In 2006, he won 17 games with the Tigers. And fans adored him as they often chanted, "Kenny! Kenny!"

MANDI WRIGHT

Roger that!

IN 2006, IN A TOWN THAT ONCE BOOED HIM, KENNY ROGERS HAS MADE A RECOVERY

By Michael Rosenberg

In 2005, Kenny Rogers was the talk of baseball.

He threw a camera to the ground and sent a cameraman to the hospital.

It wasn't terribly violent — athletes are arrested for worse every week — but it was still wrong. Rogers, who was pitching for the Texas Rangers at the time, admitted he "should have acted professionally."

And maybe the incident would have passed, but it was televised. Again and again.

And pretty soon, everyone had something to say about Kenny Rogers. He was even booed at the All-Star Game at Comerica Park.

This is about a person's entire life being seen through the prism of his worst minutes of behavior.

In 2006, Rogers started the All-Star Game and led a young pitching staff to the World Series.

JULIAN H. GONZALEZ

Rogers arrived in Detroit with the worst postseason ERA (8.85) of any pitcher ever. But he was exceptional in the 2006 playoffs.

Rogers advised fellow left-hander Mike Maroth to throw off the third-base side of the pitching rubber. Maroth responded with the best numbers of his career (before getting injured).

Rogers showed right-hander

Jeremy Bonderman a different grip for his change-up.

Left-hander Nate Robertson picked Rogers' brain about how to pitch with runners on base.

Has Rogers really helped that much?

"Absolutely," Robertson said. "We haven't had the veteran presence that has had that kind of success, and a guy that's been approachable like Kenny has been. It's just been a thrill."

Rogers endured 18 seasons and won his 200th game this season, yet he had never enjoyed the rapture of October success.

Until now.

"I'm sure there were plenty of people who didn't think I was capable of something like this," Rogers said after career games against the Yankees and A's in the postseason. "But that's also a reflection of what we've gone through as a team. Nobody expected us to get as far as we have."

Arizona Diamondbacks outfielder Eric Byrnes, a regular on the Fox postseason pregame show, had an interesting take after watching a tape of Rogers pitching in the playoffs.

"Watching that video freaks me out," Byrnes said. "Kenny Rogers is possessed. This guy, I felt like he was going to jump through that camera and come out and get me. This is 'Poltergeist' stuff."

JULIAN H. GONZALEZ

Kenny Rogers gets a hug from his wife, Rebecca, after his victory in Game 3 of the ALDS. It was his first victory over the Yankees since 1993.

KENNY ROGERS

LEFT-HANDED PITCHER

Age: 41   **From:** Savannah, Ga.

Ht/wt: 6-1, 190   **Experience:** 18 years   **2006 salary:** $8,000,000

The role: A bargain ace who started the All-Star Game and led a young pitching staff.

NOTABLE
▪ One of the best-fielding pitchers and has a great pick-off move.
▪ Nickname is "The Gambler" after country music star Kenny Rogers' trademark single "The Gambler."
▪ Only Tiger besides Pudge Rodriguez with World Series experience entering the season.

STATS
W-L 17-8
IP 204
BB.......... 62
K 99
ERA 3.84

Just in time

LIKELY ROOKIE OF THE YEAR
JUSTIN VERLANDER
POWERS TIGERS' ROTATION

By Jon Paul Morosi

Throughout spring training, Justin Verlander's name was associated with Jeremy Bonderman, Joel Zumaya and Jordan Tata. All are hard-throwing right-handers. All are 24 or younger.

But Verlander stands out. He was named the team's fifth starter less than two years after the Tigers drafted him second overall.

And in his first full season, the kid blew the roof off expectations. He probably will be named American League rookie of the year. He is projected as the eventual staff ace.

Uncharted waters? Not long ago, Verlander was riding in buses and eat-

AMY LEANG

When Virginia-born Justin Verlander went to New York during the playoffs, he visited "Saks, a little Fifth Avenue, whatever, just walking around. I didn't buy anything there, I was just looking," he said.

Justin Verlander doesn't throw as hard as fellow rookie Joel Zumaya. But he topped out at 100 m.p.h. in the postseason.

KIRTHMON F. DOZIER

KIRTHMON F. DOZIER

Verlander celebrates with fans after the Tigers beat the Yankees in Game 4 of the ALDS. "You dream about stuff like this, but you never expect that it would happen to you," he said of the playoffs.

ing at the Steak 'n Egg. He began last year at Class A. The year before that, he was a junior at Old Dominion University in his home state. Most people can't tell you where Old Dominion is. But they can tell you it's a long way from the World Series.

Which, of course, is where the Tigers landed this year — with Verlander in the rotation.

Verlander got there with the help of his father, Richard, a former union president in Richmond, Va. Richard Verlander salvaged perhaps the most important negotiation in his family's history — Justin's contract with the Tigers — in an unofficial role. After talks had broken down, Richard revived them.

Richard also buys, fixes and drives muscle cars.

"The stars aligned," Richard Verlander said. "Unions, cars. Seems perfect."

"We're a blue-collar family. And he's a blue-collar kid. Justin fits in Detroit."

Like many Michiganders, Justin finds escape on the golf course. He is quite good, thanks in part to an extended driver that, his father said, "looks like a rake." The first time Verlander played golf, he sank a three-wood from 215 yards out.

Birdie.

His father seems confident his success on the golf course and the baseball field will continue, without changing him. He remembers something a scout told him before the draft.

"He told me that, in 10 years, the only difference about Justin will be the car he drives," Richard recalled. "I thought it was a nice compliment. The point is, he's grounded."

"He really doesn't think he should be anything special. That's the way he thinks. I'm his dad. I'm proud of that."

JUSTIN VERLANDER RIGHT-HANDED PITCHER   **Age:** 23   **From:** Manakin-Sabot, Va.

Ht/wt: 6-5, 200   **Experience:** 1 year   **2006 salary:** $980,000

The role: Has emerged as one of the most promising pitchers in baseball.

NOTABLE

■ Fastball reaches upper 90s. "He's special because he has stuff few pitchers have at any age. But what's really remarkable is how he's competed at this level as a young pitcher," Kenny Rogers said.

■ The second overall pick in the 2004 draft.

■ One of the top candidates for AL rookie of the year.

STATS

W-L 17-9
IP 186
BB.......... 60
K 124
ERA 3.63

Kenny Rogers lifts the cap off Jeremy Bonderman to show Bonderman's shaved head as Justin Verlander watches. "Plaid shirt, boots, blue jeans," Gene Bonderman says about his son's style. "He still drives trucks. He loves his Ford."

Family, Fords and fastballs

TIGERS STARTER JEREMY BONDERMAN STAYS TRUE TO SMALL-TOWN ROOTS

By Jon Paul Morosi

When Jeremy Bonderman left the clubhouse wearing a gray hooded sweat-shirt and sweatpants after a recent game, one teammate joked that Bonderman looked like he was heading out to shovel the driveway.

"Plaid shirt, boots, blue jeans," Gene Bonderman says of his son's off-field standbys. "He's true to himself. He says, 'This is who I am.' He doesn't let it get to his head.

"He still drives trucks. He loves his Ford."

Jeremy Bonderman is good at his chosen vocation — right-handed pitcher for the Tigers.

But no matter the success, he remains down-to-earth, say those who know him.

He is 23 years old. He goes to work, does his job and goes home to his wife and baby girl. He likes to hunt. He likes to fish. And, apparently, he

SCOTT COHEN/SPECIAL TO THE FREE PRESS

Tigers pitcher Jeremy Bonderman's parents, Delores and Gene, take in Detroit's game at Seattle on April 21. Bonderman grew up in Pasco, Wash.

> "I used to love Rasheed (Wallace). North Carolina was my favorite team. ... I (still) like watching him."
> ▌JEREMY BONDERMAN, on his love for basketball. He almost played in a league under NBA coach George Karl.

JULIAN H. GONZALEZ

Bonderman likes to hunt, fish and play for the Tigers. "I'm proud to be here, to wear the Olde English D," Bonderman said. "I want Mr. Kaline and all of those guys to be proud of the way we play."

SPECIAL TO THE FREE PRESS

Jeremy Bonderman, pictured at age 9, "had fire in his eyes" even during Little League, says friend Doug Vincent.

er have enabled Bonderman to become a very good starter. A reliable change-up, which he is developing, could make him great.

Bonderman's family has its own hardball history. Jeremy's grandfather, Iven, showed him how to make his fastball run — by putting pressure on one finger — when he was 12. Josh Bonderman, Jeremy's older brother, was his catcher for one high school season.

There are four Bonderman boys: Josh, Jeremy, Jeff and John. All are athletic — and, from what Jeremy says, somewhat mischievous.

"Our parents got calls," Jeremy says. "We weren't angels by any means."

loves his Ford.

Bonderman grew up in Pasco, Wash., about 225 miles southeast of Seattle. He remains a home-town hero. He lives there in the off-season. He takes the same hunting and fishing trips — with the same friends — he has since he was a boy.

Bonderman qualified for the major league draft after his junior year of high school because he dropped out to obtain his GED.

He made the majors ahead of schedule because he had enough talent to be one of the Tigers' five best pitchers in 2003. He went 6-19 as a rookie.

A hard fastball and biting slid-

JEREMY BONDERMAN   RIGHT-HANDED PITCHER   **Age:** 23   **From:** Pasco, Wash.

Ht/wt: 6-2, 220   **Experience:** 4 years   **2006 salary:** $2,300,000

The role: He looked like an ace at various times, returned to form in postseason.

NOTABLE

▪ The Oakland A's, under GM Billy Beane, selected Bonderman with the 26th overall pick in the 2001 draft. Beane later shipped Bonderman to Detroit in a three-team deal with the Yankees.
▪ An avid outdoorsman, once shot a goose from 115 yards away.
▪ Bonderman battled dyslexia during high school.

STATS

W-L 14-8
IP 214
BB 64
K 202
ERA 4.08

Nate Robertson eggs on John Judd of Wayne during a bubble-blowing contest in Garden City. Robertson's gum-chewing ritual is now an epidemic. He's also been a hit on the mound, dropping his ERA from 4.90 in 2004 to 3.84 in 2006.

Bubble, bubble

FOR OPPOSING TEAMS, NATE ROBERTSON MEANS TROUBLE

By Jon Paul Morosi

They parked their cars on Pardo Street in Garden City, around the corner from the Fanatic U sporting goods store. They waited in a line that wrapped around the building.

Many held a Sharpie in one hand and a package of Big League Chew in the other.

It's Gum Time.

At least, that's what Nate Robertson's T-shirt told them.

Gum Time began one night in May when the Tigers played the Yankees at Comerica Park, and Robertson shoved shred after shred of gum — designed to

FAMOUS BUBBLES

- The Silverdome
- Bubble Wrap
- Bubbles, the Powerpuff Girl
- Bubble tea
- Bubble baths
- On the bubble: Michigan's NCAA basketball hopes
- Scrubbing Bubbles: They work hard so you don't have to
- Bubbles, the chimpanzee
- "Tiny Bubbles"
- The Boy in the Plastic Bubble
- Big League Chew bubble gum

JULIAN H. GONZALEZ

In order to spark a Tigers rally, Nate Robertson stuffs his mouth full of Big League Chew. "It's Gum Time" became part of the Tigers' mystique.

imitate chewing tobacco — into his mouth. The Tigers rallied to force extra innings as Robertson's jaw ached. A phenomenon was born.

After that, Robertson ceased being the Tigers' bespectacled left-hander. He instead became "Big Nate Chew."

But he also is a pitcher who aggressively attacks the strike zone with a moving fastball that touches the low-to-mid-90s.

In June, Robertson shut out the defending National League champion Houston Astros in a superb seven-inning performance for which he was rewarded with a victory. Manager Jim Leyland said: "His confidence level is up a lot. His maturity is up a lot. He's made tremendous progress."

The loser that night owns more victories than any other pitcher alive. Robertson tucked away the lineup card for safekeeping.

"It's special," Robertson said of the white cardboard sheet that bore the name CLEMENS. "I'll hold on to that."

"He was pitch-for-pitch with a Hall of Famer," admired fellow pitcher Zach Miner.

Then again, something else might have been at work that night against Roger Clemens. Robertson was finished after the top of the seventh. The Tigers needed to score in the bottom of the inning for him to remain the pitcher of record.

Just then, gum started circulating. The Tigers' other starters were chewing in the dugout. In the stands, his wife, Kristin, and her friends — many of whom were wearing "It's Gum Time" shirts — began passing a bag of Big League Chew down the row.

"We were chewing," she said, "and then we got three runs."

JULIAN H. GONZALEZ

Nate Robertson carries balls to the field for batting practice. He says he used to take baseball too seriously. He once took time out of his honeymoon to talk baseball with a Tigers coach.

NATE ROBERTSON

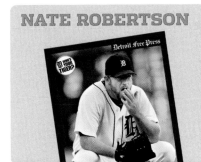

LEFT-HANDED PITCHER   **Age:** 29   **From:** Wichita, Kan.

Ht/wt: 6-2, 225   **Experience:** 3 years   **2006 salary:** $402,500

The role: The most reliable — and, at times, exceptional — starter in the 2006 season.

NOTABLE

- He started the first postseason game for the Tigers since Doyle Alexander started Game 5 against Minnesota in the 1987 ALCS.
- Father, Dick Robertson, is a retired U.S. serviceman. He builds and maintains baseball diamonds near the family's Wichita, Kan., home. One is named Robertson Field.

STATS	
W-L	...13-13
IP	.......208²/₃
BB	67
K	137
ERA	.....3.84

Premium gas

IT'S WHAT MAKES JOEL ZUMAYA GO

By Shawn Windsor

The man with the golden arm rolled up to the valet in a white SUV with tricked-out rims and a thumping bass line. He climbed out, tossed the keys to the attendant, and strode into one of the swankiest steakhouses in Oakland County wearing checkered Vans shoes, shorts and a white T-shirt.

Joel Zumaya wanted a piece of meat. And when you can throw a baseball 102 m.p.h., a table is always ready, even when you're dressed for a Southern California beach.

"Dude," he said as he stood in the lobby of the restaurant, "I just need a big table in the back."

"The recognition? It's cool," he said. "But sometimes you need your space."

Before this season, nobody knew who

MANDI WRIGHT

Joel Zumaya considers tattoos addictive. "I've always wanted a tattoo, and I waited 21 years to get one," he said. "My mom and dad don't really like 'em, but I went off and ended up getting them."

FASTER THAN A ...

How Joel Zumaya's 103-m.p.h. fastball compares to:

- Space shuttle
17,000 m.p.h.

- Lightning bolt
224,000 m.p.h.

- Peregrine falcon
200 m.p.h.

- NASCAR stock car
186 m.p.h.

- Andy Roddick serve
155 m.p.h.

- Al Iafrate slap shot
105 m.p.h.

- Amtrak train
125-150 m.p.h.

- Millennium Force
roller coaster
93 m.p.h.

- Running cheetah
70 m.p.h.

- Pass in football
45 m.p.h.

- Speeding bullet
2,700 m.p.h.

- Superman⁕
60,000 m.p.h.

⁕Superman's speed is of great debate on the Internet. Some have argued Superman can break the speed of light (about 186,000 miles per second, or 670 million m.p.h.)

Joel Zumaya gives his trademark fist pump after getting a big out. Said Kenny Rogers: "I think every guy on this team loves to watch him go out there with his high intensity stuff. It's very satisfying to watch a guy overpower people when you can't do it."

KIRTHMON F. DOZIER

JULIAN H. GONZALEZ

Joel Zumaya became one of the most recognizable faces on the Tigers. He is fond of goatees and Southern California beach chic, all while cutting a 103 m.p.h. path to the plate.

SPECIAL TO THE FREE PRESS

Zumaya, then 13, stands in front of a Mexican restaurant with mom Yvonne after his eighth-grade graduation. Zumaya still calls his mother about five times a day.

he was. Then he began running in from the bullpen with the loudspeaker blaring Jimi Hendrix, stalking the mound, striking out the best hitters in the game, taking the crowd on a vicarious ride with the radar gun.

"When I get in between those lines, a switch turns on," he explained. "It's like I'm filled with premium gas, $3 gas, dude. It pumps me up. Sometimes, to tell you the truth, I get too pumped up."

And when the 21-year-old needs time to chill — that means fishing, playing guitar on a video game or dinner with his buddies, usually with a beer and a nice cut of meat.

The legend of Zumaya started with a lime. He was 15 at the time, standing in the street in front of his house in Chula Vista, Calif., near San Diego. A block away stood a church.

He held the lime in his hand, heaved it into the air and watched it disappear. It landed on the other side of the church.

He was always throwing things then, especially at cars — especially eggs.

"I was a troublemaker," Zumaya said. "I was a punk. I did a few things I regret."

Baseball saved him, along with his mom and dad.

"We were low-class, didn't have much," he said. "But they did everything they could to provide spikes, shoes, gloves. They also taught me how to be a man, and how not to back down from anything."

The Tigers signed him in 2002 and sent him to rookie ball.

He discovered yoga. Through some sort of muscle-loosening alchemy, he arrived back with a stronger arm.

Suddenly, the fastball started hitting the 90s, and he rose up through the system. He got to spring training this year and became a fearsome 100-m.p.h. reliever.

Said Kenny Rogers: "That's what makes him Zoomy."

JOEL ZUMAYA

RIGHT-HANDED RELIEVER   **Age:** 21   **From:** Chula Vista, Calif.

Ht/wt: 6-3, 210   **Experience:** 1 year   **2006 salary:** $327,000

The role: Pitches in close games, and often comes in when a strikeout is needed.

NOTABLE
- Loves tattoos. Has an Aztec symbol on his left shoulder and another with last name going through a cross on his left arm.
- Has collected autographs of many of the players he strikes out.
- Nickname is "Zoom Zoom." "When I get in between those lines, a switch turns on," Zumaya says, on coming into a game.

STATS

W-L	6-3
IP	$83\frac{1}{3}$
BB	42
K	97
ERA	1.94

Todd Jones runs in the stands before a playoff game against the A's at Oakland. "Eighty percent of the season we were beating teams' butts every night, and we didn't know why," he said.

Out of the pen

TODD JONES OFFERS AN INSIDER'S VIEW OF THE TIGERS

Todd Jones is one of the most endearing, humorous personalities on the Tigers. He signed a two-year, $11-million contract before the 2006 season to be the Tigers' closer. He also wrote a weekly column for The Mitt, the Detroit Free Press' Sunday baseball special section. Some highlights from his columns:

A TYPICAL DAY IN THE CLUBHOUSE

For most of the players, the day starts around 3 p.m. Our batting practice for a home night game is at 4:55 p.m. In between, some guys do fan mail. The funniest thing is watching Nate Robertson get packs of Big League Chew. He signs all of them and sends them back. Some guys are working on their bats. Others are in the weight room or video room.

WANT TO HECKLE ME? BE ORIGINAL

On the road, we get yelled at for a living. Believe me, it doesn't bother us. Most of it is the same old stuff: My mom this, my wife that, hey

Todd Jones took Tigers fans on a roller coaster of emotions, but almost always came through with the save.

KIRTHMON F. DOZIER

you guys suck. Those don't get any responses from us.

If you're going to rag on us, be creative. I've been asked in New York for a ball from the bleacher bums in rightfield. After politely telling them that I didn't have one, they said, "That's OK, Jones, I'll get one when you pitch."

Just don't cuss, fans. There are kids around. You have no shot of staying in the ballpark if you swear.

LIFE ON THE PLANE

Mr. Ilitch has one plane for his two teams, the Red Wings and Tigers. Usually, the two teams' schedules don't conflict. The plane has 53 seats. All are leather, first-class captain's chairs.

There are four sets of four chairs that face each other near the back of the plane. Those are for serious card games. The manager and coaches get the front eight seats. The middle of the plane is where the rookies sit. They have no choice but to sit side-by-side so the old guys can sit with enough room in the back of the plane. We have just about every-

thing we need to eat on the flight. Not airplane food. I'm talking steak and lasagna and chicken and sandwiches. I've even had sushi.

RAIN DELAY FUN

Ever wonder what happens during rain delays? The only guy who has a bad time is the starting pitcher. He's antsy, he paces.

If the game is delayed at the start, the home team's general manager decides whether to call off the game.

A lot goes into his decision. For most clubs, a sellout means making about $1 million on tickets, food and parking. So it's not easy to just bag the game. And if bad weather is coming, the GM might try to play a game that he normally would postpone.

To kill time, in the Tigers' clubhouse, there are about 15 to 20 television sets. There's video to watch of the opposing team. There's a great food room, couches, saunas, Xboxes, you name it. If you have to kill time, this is the place to do it.

TODD JONES

RIGHT-HANDED CLOSER　　Age: 38　　From: Marietta, Ga.

Ht/wt: 6-3, 230　　Experience: 13 years　　2006 salary: $5,809,159

The role: Was one of the best closers in the AL. Converted 37 of 43 save opportunities.

NOTABLE
- Second stint as the Tigers' closer. Became the team's all-time saves leader, passing Mike Henneman, who had 154.
- Finished tied for fourth in the American League in saves, behind the Angels' Francisco Rodriguez (47), Chicago's Bobby Jenks (41) and Toronto's B.J. Ryan (38).

STATS

SV	37
IP	64
BB	11
K	28
ERA	3.94

In his Free Press column, Todd Jones credited the rookies for the Tigers' success. "(Joel) Zumaya and Justin Verlander contributed to probably 25 to 30 victories," he wrote.

Teammates say Magglio Ordonez has always been quick with a smile. He's pleasant, but quiet, and is reluctant to become the center of attention.

JULIAN H. GONZALEZ

Magg-nificent!

HE'S HUMBLE, SIMPLE AND HAS AN INTERESTING HAIRSTYLE. HE'S ALSO THE TIGERS' TOP-PAID PLAYER. HE'S MAGGLIO ORDONEZ

By Jo-Ann Barnas

Magglio Ordonez is in the second year of a five-year, $75-million contract — the richest in Tigers history. And yet, as the centerpiece of a team remarkably devoid of clashing egos, he is the player many fans know least about.

"Everyone always asks, 'How is it to play with Pudge?'" said centerfielder Curtis Granderson. "No one really says, 'How's it to play with Magglio?' I'm not really sure if people forget that he batted great for such a long time. ... He kind of flies under the radar for whatever reason."

Only the most observant fans at Comerica Park have caught on to the ritual, how Granderson and Ordonez often warm up between innings by imitating the pitcher on the mound for the Tigers or their opponent.

"He does a good Todd Jones," Granderson said of Ordonez.

Ordonez isn't a wallflower — although he often likes to dine alone on trips. He is known for his sophisticated style. He has a fondness for wristwatches, collects wine and is a particular fan of Italian reds such as Barolo. He likes to play dominoes.

KIRTHMON F. DOZIER

Brandon Inge said no one gives Magglio Ordonez "the respect that he deserves." Ordonez led the team in RBIs.

But what's with the hair?

Ordonez's loose, dark curls that peeked out from under his cap this season haven't seen a pair of scissors in months. "My wife likes it," Ordonez said.

"I say, 'I'm going to cut it.' She says, 'No, no, no!' "

Walk into the Tigers clubhouse today, and you'll find Ordonez's gift: a leather massage chair.

The chair, which he bought "for around $5,000," he said, has the Tigers' emblem on the headrest.

Ordonez said any player can enjoy it and they often do.

"It's nice," shortstop Carlos Guillen said. "No sign-up. I use it all the time."

Earlier this season, Ordonez confessed to a Chicago newspaper that he was emotional when he watched his former teammates win the World Series last year.

How emotional? He cried. Deep down, he never wanted to leave Chicago.

"I left because of business," he said. "I spent my whole career there. I left a year early, and they won the World Series. But I turn the page."

Ordonez's voice turned more serious.

"For the Tigers, I want to accomplish going to the playoffs and win the whole thing."

JULIAN H. GONZALEZ

Magglio Ordonez makes a running catch at Minnesota. After an injury-riddled Detroit debut in 2005. Ordonez enjoyed a strong first half and made the All-Star team.

THE BIG SLUGGERS

How Magglio Ordonez compared with the highest-paid hitters in the majors. ✳ Salary in millions.

Player	Pos.	Team	Salary✳	H	HR	RBI	SO	AVG
Alex Rodriguez	3B	NYY	$25.7	166	35	121	139	.290
Derek Jeter	SS	NYY	$20.6	214	14	97	102	.343
Jason Giambi	1B	NYY	$20.4	113	37	113	106	.253
Barry Bonds	OF	S.F.	$20	99	26	77	51	.270
Jeff Bagwell	1B	Hou.	$19.4	Did not play this season				
Manny Ramirez	OF	Bos.	$18.3	144	35	102	102	.321
Todd Helton	1B	Col.	$16.6	165	15	81	64	.302
Magglio Ordonez	**OF**	**Det.**	**$16.2**	**177**	**24**	**104**	**87**	**.298**
Lance Berkman	1B/OF	Hou.	$14.5	169	45	136	106	.315
Jim Thome	DH	CWS	$14.2	141	42	109	147	.288

MAGGLIO ORDONEZ

RIGHTFIELDER	Age: 32	From: Caracas, Venezuela
Ht/wt: 6-0, 215	Experience: 9 years	2006 salary: $16,200,000

The role: Tigers' power-hitting cleanup man, leading run-producer. Quiet, dangerous.

NOTABLE
- Ordonez and Curtis Granderson often warm up between innings by imitating the pitcher for the Tigers or their opponent.
- Father Maglio gave his son an extra "g" for good luck.
- Five-time All-Star, finished eighth in MVP voting in 2002 (38 HRs, 135 RBIs, .320 AVG).

STATS
AB.........593
R 82
HR...........24
RBI........104
AVG .... .298

Fan favorite Pudge Rodriguez celebrates after hitting a two-out, two-run homer in the bottom of the ninth to beat the Indians in August.

Pudge factor

GOOD TIMES FINALLY CAUGHT UP WITH CATCHER IVAN (PUDGE) RODRIGUEZ

By Jo-Ann Barnas

Catcher Pudge Rodriguez learned how to play the game as a child on the streets of Vega Baja, Puerto Rico, improvising with a stick and wad of tape with his older brother, Jose.

He then became an All-Star during his 12 seasons with the Texas Rangers and later won a World Series with the Florida Marlins in 2003.

So Rodriguez was lauded as the most important Tigers free-agent signing when he arrived in Detroit in February 2004 for a four-year contract worth $40 million.

But the 2005 season had proved to be among the most difficult of his career.

Jose Canseco's published book accused Rodriguez of steroid use while with the Rangers. Rumors flared when Rodriguez came to spring training 22 pounds lighter. He strenuously denied the accusations.

He batted .276, his lowest average since 1993. The losing got to him. He clashed with then-manager Alan Trammell. And his marriage to his wife, Maribel, ended in divorce.

"It affected his focus at that time," Tigers president and general manager Dave Dombrowski said. "We knew it ... was not a traditional Pudge year."

AMY LEANG

Pudge Rodriguez bounced back from a subpar 2005 season. He steered the pitching staff like a ship's captain. And his defense was exceptional.

But with the arrival of a new manager, Jim Leyland, came a new attitude, a fresh start. After the Tigers beat the Yankees in the American League Division Series, Rodriguez turned the festive atmosphere into a dance party, calling out: "We need music!"

His teammates consider Rodriguez a leader of the team. Rodriguez considers them brothers.

"All of us are very close," Rodriguez said. "And when you have that on a baseball team, you're going to go a long way."

This season was different. Rodriguez has steered the pitching staff like a ship's captain. And his defense was exceptional.

Named to the All-Star team for the 13th time, Rodriguez topped all catchers by throwing out 45.7% of runners attempting to steal. He led all AL catchers with a .998 fielding percentage — his two errors the fewest by any AL catcher with a minimum of 100 games caught.

"Pudge is probably the best catcher I've ever been fortunate enough to pitch to — and the most talented by far," Kenny Rogers said.

Said Mike Maroth: "That's why he's a future Hall of Famer."

PUDGE RODRIGUEZ

CATCHER		Age: 34	From: Vega Baja, Puerto Rico
Ht/Wt: 5-9, 190		Experience: 15 years	2006 salary: $10,616,410

The role: Deters base-stealing, counted on to lead fairly inexperienced playoff team.

NOTABLE
- Selected to MLB's Latino Legends team.
- Started at first base for the first time in his career May 9 against the Baltimore Orioles.
- An All-Star Game starter for the 13th time this season, most among active players, and the most All-Star starts at catcher.

STATS

AB	547
R	74
HR	13
RBI	69
AVG	.300

KIRTHMON F. DOZIER

Pudge Rodriguez was named to the All-Star team for the 13th time. He topped all catchers by throwing out 45.7% of runners attempting to steal in the regular season.

Señor Cycle

CARLOS GUILLEN TAUGHT TIGERS FANS A NEW EXPRESSION IN AUGUST

By Jon Paul Morosi

El ciclo.

It means "the cycle" in his native Venezuela. He became the 10th Tiger to hit for the cycle in a 10-4 victory over the Tampa Bay Devil Rays at Tropicana Field on Aug. 1.

The cycle brought him acclaim on domestic sports highlight shows and made front-page news in his home country.

It seemed appropriate that Guillen's feat came on the night the Tigers won their 71st game, matching their total from 2005. Guillen's consistent presence in the lineup — after missing nearly half the games last year — has been a big factor behind the Tigers' most successful season in two decades.

Although he hasn't been great defensively (he led American League shortstops in errors), Guillen might be the club's top all-around offensive player.

Carlos Guillen laughs in the Tigers' clubhouse as Pudge Rodriguez, left, relaxes next to him. Guillen is considered a leader for the Tigers' Hispanic players.

ERIC SEALS

KIRTHMON F. DOZIER

Guillen, like Craig Monroe, had several clutch home runs this season, including this walk-off blast in July against Kansas City.

The fact that Guillen led the team in stolen bases with 20 (a favorite measure of traditional baseball observers) and on-base percentage (the sacred statistic of sabermetricians) suggests his play is a fusion of the many skills that

MANDI WRIGHT

Carlos Guillen smiles after a double against the Yankees in the playoffs. He batted .571 in the first round.

make a baseball team go.

Guillen plays hurt. He calms pitchers. He encourages teammates. Among shortstops, that's second only to Kalamazoo's Derek Jeter.

"These are like your brothers, your family," Guillen said. "This is your job, but you have to have fun, talk, enjoy what you're doing. That's the way I like it. I want to help my teammates any way I can."

Amaury Pi-Gonzalez, the Spanish-language broadcaster for Guillen's former team, the Seattle Mariners, noticed on a visit to the clubhouse this season how the team's Latin American players were drawn to Guillen.

They were watching the World Cup final that day and predicting whether France or Italy would win. Guillen, as usual, was in the middle of the conversation.

"He's great," Pi-Gonzalez said. "He was the leader of that group. All the other players were around Carlos Guillen."

Guillen will be a free agent after the 2007 season, but there's a good chance that he would consider staying. "I feel good here," he said. "I like Detroit."

CARLOS GUILLEN

SHORTSTOP

Ht/wt: 6-1, 213

Age: 31   **From:** Maracay, Venezuela

Experience: 8 years   **2006 salary:** $5,000,000

The role: He is the Tigers' most essential hitter. Leads the team in walks.

NOTABLE
▐ Led the team in average, runs and stolen bases.
▐ Played first base for Venezuela in this year's World Baseball Classic.
▐ Is known for using his teammates' bats instead of his own.

STATS
AB 543
R 100
HR 19
RBI......... 85
AVG .... .320

> "He's the MVP of the ALCS. He's one of those guys you have to watch, day in and day out, to appreciate."
>
> ■ Tigers president and general manager **DAVE DOMBROWSKI**, on Placido Polanco

JULIAN H. GONZALEZ

Placido Polanco slides safely into third base in Game 4 against New York. "Go to Google and look up 'baseball player,' " said Andy Van Slyke, the Tigers' first-base coach. "His name would be on the top Web page."

Polanco power

THE TIGERS GOT A HECK OF A DEAL WHEN THEY TRADED FOR ALCS MVP PLACIDO POLANCO

By Jon Paul Morosi

Placido Polanco stood quietly in one corner of the moist Tigers clubhouse following the 6-3, American League Championship-clinching victory over the Oakland Athletics. He had a bottle of G.H. Mumm champagne in his hand, a cigar in his mouth and his wife at his side.

He didn't say much. He didn't need to. His performance had been sufficiently booming for all to hear.

Polanco batted .529 (9-for-17) in four ALCS games. Without Polanco, Magglio Ordonez doesn't bat in the ninth inning of Game 4 and doesn't hit the game-winning home run.

Placido Polanco makes a diving stop in Game 2 of the ALCS against Oakland. He batted .529 (9-for-17) in four games and was named MVP of the series.

JULIAN H. GONZALEZ

Placido Polanco rarely strikes out, gets big hits and never disappoints. "I never saw him give an at-bat away this whole year, and I can't say that about too many guys who went to the plate over 500 times in the big leagues," said Andy Van Slyke, the Tigers' first-base coach.

KIRTHMON F. DOZIER

And, as usual, Polanco turned numerous double plays at second base.

Polanco, underappreciated by all but those who watch him closely, was voted the ALCS most valuable player.

"Go to Google and look up 'baseball player,' " suggested first-base coach Andy Van Slyke. "His name would be on the top Web page.

"To me, baseball's not about the big things. It's the little things that add up. Moving a guy over. Getting the base hit with two outs and a man on first. I never saw him give an at-bat away this whole year, and I can't say that about too many guys who went to the plate over 500 times in the big leagues."

And don't forget that Polanco missed 5½ weeks with a separated left shoulder, returning with a

week left in the regular season. Some wondered whether he would return this season at all. In fact, in a moment of frustration, Polanco said he was finished for the season.

Polanco came to symbolize so much about these Tigers. His previous team, the Philadelphia Phillies, traded him because they wanted Chase Utley to play every day. Fine. Dave Dombrowski, the Tigers' president and general manager, was happy to take him. Dombrowski was asked how important the acquisition of Polanco for Ugueth Urbina and Ramon Martinez had been.

The first word out of his mouth: "Huge."

"He's the MVP of the ALCS," Dombrowski said. "He's one of those guys you have to watch, day in and day out, to appreciate. He's a professional. He does everything well."

PLACIDO POLANCO

SECOND BASEMAN
Ht/wt: 5-10, 194

Age: 31   **From:** Santo Domingo, Dominican Republic
Experience: 8 years   **2006 salary:** $4,600,000

The role: A key hitter who makes solid contact and rarely strikes out.

NOTABLE
▪ Played prep basketball in the Dominican Republic.
▪ Known as "Poli" by his teammates.
▪ Struck out only once every 22.04 plate appearances in 2005 — best among all major league players.

STATS
AB 461
R 58
HR 4
RBI 52
AVG ... .295

Meet Mr. Clutch

TIMELY HITTING FROM CRAIG MONROE QUIETS THE WHISPERING NAYSAYERS

By Shawn Windsor

Willie Horton once got so mad at him he hurled a bottle at a television in his home, shattering a 62-inch screen. Craig Monroe didn't know it at the time. He found out later, when Horton left a message on his cell phone telling Monroe that he owed him several thousand dollars because a poor swing made him lose his temper.

Horton was joking. Sort of.

All Horton knew was that Monroe, a player of immense talent whom Horton had taken under his wing — and the Tiger who most reminded him of himself — didn't have his head where it needed to be.

"You don't go out there and look for some angel in the sky," Horton explained.

"Those guys stay in a slump all year."

For three years, Monroe teased the club with his pop and rocket arm. He started slowly in 2006, too, until he found a groove and asserted himself as the team's most eminent clutch hitter in recent memory.

Monroe, 29, introspective and guarded, originally signed with the Texas Rangers. After years of struggles and a brief stint in the majors, the team released him. The Tigers claimed him off waivers.

Baseball kept him from a formal higher education, but he became fluent in Spanish in the minors. Monroe wanted to connect to some of his Latino teammates. He liked the free spirit many Latinos seemed to bring.

Craig Monroe, the guy some fans wanted to replace, takes a bow before a cheering crowd after hitting the Tigers' first grand slam of the season against Chicago in July.

Craig Monroe points to the stands after hitting a home run against the A's in the ALCS. The Tigers shopped for outfielders at the trading deadline, but were glad they stuck with the productive Monroe.

JULIAN H. GONZALEZ

Craig Monroe, 29, introspective and guarded, has spent a lifetime trying to make himself matter in the big leagues. In 2006, he started to do it.

KIRTHMON F. DOZIER

CRAIG IN THE CLUTCH

Craig Monroe's game-winning heroics in the 2006 regular season:

■ **May 25 at Kansas City:** Hit go-ahead solo homer in ninth off Elmer Dessens to complete a rally from a 6-0 hole; the Tigers scored four more in ninth for a 13-8 victory.

■ **June 27 vs. Houston:** Hit winning double in the seventh off Dan Wheeler to give Nate Robertson the victory, Roger Clemens the loss.

■ **July 19 vs. White Sox:** Hit grand slam in the sixth off Javier Vazquez to turn a 2-1 deficit into a 5-2 victory.

■ **July 28 at Minnesota:** Singled down the third-base line in the 10th to score Omar Infante with the winning run in a 3-2 victory.

■ **Aug. 4 vs. Cleveland:** Hit a two-out, two-run homer off Fernando Cabrera in the eighth after hitting one barely foul earlier in a 7-6 victory.

■ **Aug. 15 at Boston:** Singled in the winning run in the ninth off right-fielder Wily Mo Pena's glove for a 3-2 victory.

■ **Aug. 30 at Yankees:** Hit a three-run homer off Scott Proctor in the ninth to turn a 3-2 deficit into a 5-3 victory.

FAMOUS CRAIGS

■ "Coach" Craig T. Nelson
■ Craig David (R&B singer)
■ Craig from the "Friday" trilogy
■ Roger Craig (ex-NFLer)
■ Roger Craig ('84 Tigers pitching coach and proponent of the split-fingered fastball)
■ Craig Biggio (Astros second baseman)
■ Craig Kilborn (late-night host succeeded by, who else, Craig Ferguson)
■ Craig Krenzel (Utica Ford, Buckeyes QB, now out of pro football)
■ Craigslist (Internet classifieds)
■ Jenny Craig (weight loss centers)
■ Daniel Craig (or Bond, James Bond)

"They had a good time, they have fun, they laugh," he said. "I've kind of adopted the Latin way a little."

But there were times when he enjoyed himself too much away from the game. And then there was the incident in December 2004. After a solid season, he walked out of a Florida department store with a $29.98 belt around his waist. He was arrested for shoplifting. He later told teammates that his shirt had flapped over the belt and he had forgotten about it.

"God has a lot of ways of humbling you," he said.

Monroe agreed to enter a diversion program to have the charges dropped. But he said he didn't ever want to lose track of what that felt like.

Not for his mother, Marilyn Monroe. Not for wife Kasey or daughter Morgan, 5, who both live in Frisco, Texas. Monroe recently bought a house there.

"He is learning how to be a man in a professional game. Before he would go out and have fun and keep having fun while the game is going on," Horton said.

Part of that is manager Jim Leyland's influence.

He runs a professional clubhouse.

The biggest difference, Leyland said, is that Monroe used to think he was a good player.

Now he *knows* he is.

CRAIG MONROE

OUTFIELDER   **Age:** 29   **From:** Texarkana, Texas

Ht/wt: 6-1, 205   **Experience:** 4 years   **2006 salary:** $2,800,000

The role: He hit anywhere in the lineup, has provided offense (led the team in homers).

NOTABLE

■ Played football, was an all-state basketball player in high school.
■ Has multiple tattoos, including a cross with "Anything's possible" above it, plus one with his daughter's name, Morgan.
■ Slow start prompted Tigers to consider replacing him in leftfield through a trade.

STATS

AB	541
R	89
HR	28
RBI	92
AVG	.255

Boy wonder

FROM HIS HOME RUNS TO HIS FIELD GOALS TO HIS BATTING PRACTICE, BRANDON INGE PLAYS THE ROLE OF KID FOR THE TIGERS

By Shawn Windsor

Of all the impressive and quirky athletic feats Tigers third baseman Brandon Inge has pulled off, it was the inadvertent shot to the groin that reveals his most unheralded value to the Tigers — his inner boyishness.

Early this season he thought it might be fun to slingshot a bottle of Gatorade from Comerica Park's third-base line to deep centerfield using a belt of rubber designed to loosen muscles during pregame stretches.

Inge, 29, positioned the bottle in the improvised slingshot and let it fly. The bottle, however, shot back toward his groin.

Said Inge: "It didn't quite work out for me."

But these days, just about everything else is.

MANDI WRIGHT

Brandon Inge has endeared himself to teammates with his boyish antics and natural playing ability. "He's like a 10-year-old kid," Vance Wilson said.

He might never be the .300-hitting, relatively error-free corner infielder fans desire. (No player on the current roster attracts such

Back in '03, when he ventured into metro Detroit, Brandon Inge feared someone would recognize him and "would tell me I suck."
AMY LEANG

Inge made a diving save and a quick throw at Minnesota on July 30. "I don't know anybody that throws it better than Brandon Inge," manager Jim Leyland said.

mixed reviews among the team's most ardent followers.)

But Inge has turned third base into his own highlight reel. And his bat is beginning to catch up.

Manager Jim Leyland voted for Inge on the player-manager All-Star ballot.

"I might be biased and get a lot of arguments," Leyland said, "but I don't know anybody that throws it better than Brandon Inge."

Said reliever Joel Zumaya: "His plays are freakish, man."

Zumaya wasn't just talking about what Inge does during games. In 2005, when the Tigers were inside Ford Field for a promotional event, Inge casually kicked a 50-yard field goal. He flips and twirls bats with his feet like a soccer star.

"This really is a bunch of men playing a boys' game, and Brandon is typical of that," said backup catcher Vance Wilson. "He's like a 10-year-old kid."

There are those who would like to see Inge used as a utility guy, an athletic backup with pop. Leyland doesn't buy that.

"I disagree totally now that I've seen him. ... I think this guy has a chance, if he continues the progress rate that he's going now, to be a hell of an everyday, major league third baseman for a long time," he said.

GREAT FEATS

Some of Brandon Inge's freakish athletic feats:

- Drives 360 yards on the golf course.
- Dunks a basketball even though he's shorter than his listed 5-11 height.
- Has thrown a 95-m.p.h. fastball.
- Kicked a 50-yard field goal at Ford Field (too bad the Lions never have kicking troubles).
- Once took an aluminum bat and hit a ball over Comerica's score-board — from home plate.
- Flips and twirls bats with his feet like a soccer star. (We could have used him in the World Cup.)
- Can throw a lefty curveball with his right hand by throwing it from behind his head.

BRANDON INGE

THIRD BASEMAN **Age:** 29 **From:** Lynchburg, Va.

Ht/wt: 5-11, 188 **Experience:** 5 years **2006 salary:** $3,000,000

The role: Inge played strong defense and contributed power from the No. 9 hole.

NOTABLE

- Called up in 2001, played catcher, but struggled offensively, until 2004 after the Tigers signed Pudge Rodriguez.
- Became utility player, then a regular at third base. "I never really liked catching. Going back to the infield put me on cloud nine."
- Finished fourth among AL third basemen in homers.

STATS

AB 542
R 83
HR 27
RBI......... 83
AVG .... .253

Curtis Granderson watches BET on television at his apartment in Troy while shopping the Internet for extra World Series tickets for friends and family. He lives with Joel Zumaya. "Grandy's a sweetheart, man," Zumaya said.

Grand opening

MEET THE POLITE, GROUNDED TIGERS OUTFIELDER, CURTIS GRANDERSON

By Shawn Windsor

Curtis Granderson, the Tigers' young centerfielder, is a perfectionist.

That nature shapes most everything he does, whether it's gracefully patrolling centerfield in Comerica Park, spraying the ball with a pop that belies his pedestrian frame — he's listed at 6-feet-1 and 185 pounds — or studying the tendencies of pitchers and hitters.

But all anyone in the Tigers' clubhouse wants to talk about is how polite, mature and nice a guy Granderson is.

"I don't want this to sound

Curtis Granderson made some highlight-reel catches in centerfield. He also hit .313, with three homers and seven RBIs in the first two rounds of the playoffs.

JULIAN H. GON

When he was growing up, basketball was Curtis Granderson's favorite sport. He attended the University of Illinois-Chicago, but after an injury, he chose baseball over hoops.

SPECIAL TO THE FREE PRESS

MR. THRIFTY

Curtis Granderson might make more with a World Series bonus than his annual $335,000 salary.

But don't expect him to spend it on much.

He told USA Today that he doesn't believe in frivolities. He is business savvy — he graduated from the University of Illinois-Chicago with a double major in business management and business marketing.

He is teased by teammates about his car. He drives a basic 4-year-old blue Chevy TrailBlazer. There are players with bigger TVs in their cars than he has in his apartment. "Not too many guys in here have 24-inch TVs from Wal-Mart," he said.

He chose cloth seats instead of leather to save $1,000, even using his dad's GM discount to buy the Chevy. He lives in a two-bedroom apartment in Troy that's not too large. He shares it with teammate Joel Zumaya, spending $1,400 a month, which includes rental furniture. No plants. No major decorations — other than a 2006 Tigers schedule magnet on the refrigerator.

He also grabs roast beef sandwiches from Arby's and sugar cookies.

Hey, why not? The cookies were a two-for-one special.

weird," said reliever Joel Zumaya, Granderson's roommate, "but Grandy's a sweetheart, man."

Zumaya asked Granderson to room with him in a two-bedroom apartment in Troy. Zumaya, a burly, California born-and-raised pitcher who stalks the mound with fist-pumping menace, would appear an odd choice for the studious, low-key, midwestern Granderson.

But it works.

"Well, first thing, he's clean," Zumaya said.

The second thing?

"He's one of the coolest guys I know," he said.

Maybe it's because Granderson finished his marketing degree in his spare time after he left the University of Illinois-Chicago and signed with the Tigers in 2002.

Or because he hangs out in blues and jazz clubs. Or because he sounds like he's 40, when he's only 25.

Maybe it's because he doesn't care that people know he still lives with his parents during the off-season, or that he talks to his mother most days, or that he was an honor student in high school at Thornton Fractional South in Lynwood, a burb of Chicago.

Or maybe it's his sense of style: He favors Velcro shoes from Wal-Mart.

"If something is nice and expensive, and everybody has it, then what's the point?" he asks. "I like to be different."

And he has never felt the need to apologize for who he is or where he came from.

"Why treat what I had negatively? I was blessed," he said. "It's not a bad thing to have good parents, to have good grades."

Said Tigers manager Jim Leyland: "He knows where he's going and what he wants to do," Leyland said. "He's a real bright kid."

As for his play?

"He's got a chance to be a real good one."

CURTIS GRANDERSON   CENTERFIELDER

Age: 25   **From:** Blue Island, Ill.

Ht/wt: 6-1, 185   **Experience:** 2 years   **2006 salary:** $335,000

The role: He catalyzes the offense, defense — as the leadoff man and patrolling center.

NOTABLE

- Wrist injury kept him from playing college basketball at University of Illinois-Chicago.
- Takes batting practice to the song "Everyday I'm Hustling" by Rick Ross and various songs by NERD.
- Still lives with his parents, both teachers, in the off-season.

STATS

AB	596
R	90
HR	19
RBI	68
AVG	.260

The players

SEAN CASEY

FIRST BASEMAN

Age: 32
From: Willingsboro, N.J.
Ht/wt: 6-4, 237
Experience: 10 years
2006 salary: $8,500,000
The role: Acquired at the trade deadline from Pittsburgh, he drew walks and put the ball in play.

NOTABLE
■ In 2005, sang a version of Toby Keith's "How Do You Like Me Now?" on a CD of players/singers.
■ Nicknamed "The Mayor" because he likes to talk.
■ Big pro-wrestling fan.

STATS
AB 184
R 17
HR 5
RBI 30
AVG ... .245

OMAR INFANTE

UTILITY INFIELDER

Age: 24
From: Puerto La Cruz, Venezuela
Ht/wt: 6-0, 180
Experience: 3 years
2006 salary: $385,000
The role: Can play center-field or infield positions as a solid utility player.

NOTABLE
■ Signed with Tigers in April 1999 when he was only 17.
■ Batted .330 on the road and only .220 at home.
■ Quiet guy, who doesn't talk much with the media.

STATS
AB 224
R 35
HR 4
RBI 25
AVG ... .277

NEIFI PEREZ

UTILITY INFIELDER

Age: 33
From: Villa Mella, Dominican Republic
Ht/wt: 6-0, 175
Experience: 11 years
2006 salary: $2,500,000
The role: Perez filled in for Polanco after he suffered a separated shoulder.

NOTABLE
■ Played for Jim Leyland when he was with the Rockies.
■ Won a Gold Glove at shortstop for the Rockies in 2000.
■ Acquired from the Cubs in August.

STATS
AB 65
R 4
HR 0
RBI 5
AVG ... .200

RAMON SANTIAGO

UTILITY INFIELDER

Age: 27
From: Las Matas de Farfan, Dominican Republic
Ht/wt: 5-11, 175
Experience: 3 years
2006 salary: $375,000
The role: Played at three infield positions in utility role.

NOTABLE
■ Was traded to Seattle in 2004 for Carlos Guillen, then released, then re-signed with the Tigers.
■ Lives in same town near Haitian border as ex-Tiger Juan Encarnacion.

STATS
AB 80
R 9
HR 0
RBI 3
AVG ... .225

ALEXIS GOMEZ

OUTFIELDER

Age: 28
From: Loma de Cabrera, Dominican Republic
Ht/wt: 6-2, 180
Experience: 2 years
2006 salary: Minimum
The role: Gomez has good athletic ability and was used as pinch-runner, pinch-hitter and defensive replacement.

NOTABLE
■ Only position player on the team who throws left-handed.
■ Hit 4 HRs in one game for Triple-A Toledo.
■ Had a HR and 4 RBIs in ALCS win.

STATS
AB 103
R 17
HR 1
RBI 6
AVG ... .272

MARCUS THAMES

OUTFIELDER

Age: 29
From: Louisville, Miss.
Ht/wt: 6-2, 220
Experience: 2 years
2006 salary: $342,000
The role: Thames' first full season in the majors in a 10-year pro career was spent mostly as the starting DH.

NOTABLE
■ Served four years in the National Guard. "It made me a man," he said. "It was one of the best things I ever did. "
■ Best friends with Craig Monroe.

STATS
AB 348
R 61
HR 26
RBI 60
AVG ... .256

CHRIS SHELTON

FIRST BASEMAN

Age: 26
From: Salt Lake City
Ht/wt: 6-0, 215
Experience: 2 years
2006 salary: $365,000
The role: He was the team's Opening Day first baseman but faltered late in the season, getting sent down to Triple-A Toledo in late July.

NOTABLE
■ Started off hot (.326, 10 home runs in April) before cooling off.
■ Acquired from Pittsburgh in Rule 5 draft in 2005.

STATS
AB 373
R 50
HR 16
RBI 47
AVG ... .273

VANCE WILSON

CATCHER

Age: 33
From: Mesa, Ariz.
Ht/wt: 5-11, 215
Experience: 6 years
2006 salary: $750,000
The role: A backup at catcher and experienced game-caller.

NOTABLE
■ He met his wife on a recruiting visit to Arkansas. Wilson never played for the Razorbacks, signing with the Mets.
■ On May 17, he hit a game-winning two-run homer — the biggest of his career, he says.

STATS
AB 152
R 18
HR 5
RBI 18
AVG ... .283

The pitchers

JASON GRILLI

MIDDLE RELIEF

Age: 29
From: Royal Oak
Ht/wt: 6-5, 225
Experience: 1 year
2006 salary: $350,000
The role: Grilli can pitch long or short. He stranded 27 of 37 runners — one of the best on the team.

NOTABLE
■ Pitched for Italy in the World Baseball Classic.
■ His father, Steve, pitched for the Tigers in 1975-77.
■ Was selected by the Giants as the fourth pick in the '97 draft.

STATS
W-L 2-3
IP 62
BB 25
K 31
ERA ... 4.21

WIL LEDEZMA

SPOT STARTER

Age: 25
From: Guarico, Venezuela
Ht/wt: 6-4, 212
Experience: 2 years
2006 salary: Minimum
The role: Ledezma pitched as both a starter and reliever.

NOTABLE
■ The Tigers selected him in the 2002 Rule 5 draft.
■ Started the season with the Toledo Mud Hens along with Miner and Colon. Came up in mid-June, and he didn't allow an ER in 14 of his first 17 relief outings.

STATS
W-L 3-3
IP 60¹/₃
BB 23
K 39
ERA 3.58

ZACH MINER

SPOT STARTER

Age: 24
From: St. Louis
Ht/wt: 6-3, 200
Experience: 1 year
2006 salary: Minimum
The role: Miner went from no invitation to big-league camp, to the rotation and then to the bullpen.

NOTABLE
■ Miner was drafted by the Braves and signed for $1.25M, a record for a 4th-rounder.
■ His favorite players as a child were Andy Van Slyke, Ozzie Smith and Jack Clark.

STATS
W-L 7-6
IP 93
BB 32
K 59
ERA 4.84

FERNANDO RODNEY

SETUP MAN

Age: 29
From: Samana, Dominican Republic
Ht/wt: 5-11, 218
Experience: 3 years
2006 salary: $385,000
The role: Rodney has been a reliable setup man in his first full season after missing all of 2004 following Tommy John surgery.

NOTABLE
■ Was the closer for the Dominican Republic in the WBC.
■ Was Tigers' substitute closer early, saving seven games.

STATS
W-L 7-4
IP 71²/₃
BB 34
K 65
ERA 3.52

JAMIE WALKER

LEFTY SPECIALTY

Age: 35
From: McMinnville, Tenn.
Ht/wt: 6-2, 185
Experience: 6 years
2006 salary: $1,250,000
The role: Walker has the longest active continuous tenure in Detroit. He gets big left-handed hitters out.

NOTABLE
■ Walker has a fierce attitude and likes to joke in a folksy tone.
■ Second favorite sport is bull riding.
■ Decorates locker stall with fighter plane bullets.

STATS
W-L 0-1
IP 48
BB 8
K 37
ERA 2.81

MIKE MAROTH

LEFTY STARTER

Age: 29
From: Orlando, Fla.
Ht/wt: 6-0, 190
Experience: 4 years
2006 salary: $2,300,000
The role: Arguably the No. 1 starter until a May 25 elbow injury sidelined him for 3 months.

NOTABLE
■ Has worked numerous community-service events.
■ Said Baptist faith helped him get through 2003, when he lost 21 games. "God doesn't look at the numbers, for one thing."

STATS
W-L 5-2
IP 53²/₃
BB 16
K 24
ERA ... 4.19

ROMAN COLON

MIDDLE RELIEF

Age: 27
From: Monte Cristi, Dominican Republic
Ht/wt: 6-6, 225
Experience: 2 years
2006 salary: Minimum
The role: A long reliever who missed the final two months with back spasms.

NOTABLE
■ Youngest of nine brothers and sisters.
■ Brother Daniel was a minor-league prospect for the Dodgers.
■ Acquired along with Miner from Braves for pitcher Kyle Farnsworth in 2005.

STATS
W-L 2-0
IP 38²/₃
BB 14
K 25
ERA 4.89

ANDREW MILLER

LEFTY SPECIALTY

Age: 21
From: Gainesville, Fla.
Ht/wt: 6-6, 210
Experience: 1 year
2006 salary: Minimum
The role: Called up in August, he throws 97 m.p.h., which is rare for a left-hander.

NOTABLE
■ Pitched in the 2006 College World Series for North Carolina.
■ He was the sixth pick in 2006 amateur draft.
■ Rated No. 1 prospect by MLB.com and Baseball America.

STATS
W-L 0-1
IP 10¹/₃
BB 10
K 6
ERA ... 6.10

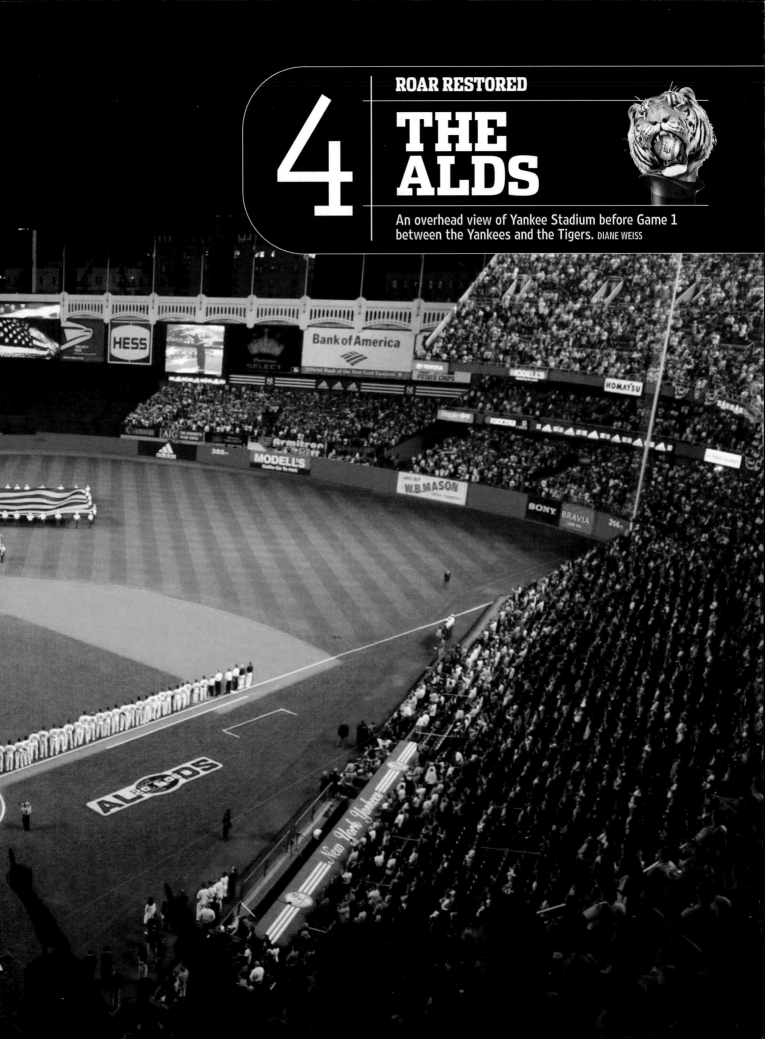

ROAR RESTORED

4 | THE ALDS

An overhead view of Yankee Stadium before Game 1 between the Yankees and the Tigers. DIANE WEISS

Roadwork ahead

A crushing defeat on final day of season but, hey, it's time to battle the Yankees

By Mitch Albom

At the end of the regular season, for the first time in more than four months, the Tigers were looking up. They were in second place. The Twins had won. They had nudged ahead of Detroit in the Central Division.

The Royals — yes, the Kansas City Royals, who had lost 100 games — completed an improbable sweep, when one Tigers victory would have given them the American League's Central Division title.

It is a strange mix of emotions; after all, Detroit is in the playoffs for the first time since 1987.

But, in the final month, the Tigers blew a six-game lead over the Twins. In the final week, they lost five in a row, all at home. This is not what they mean when they say "take some momentum into the playoffs." You don't want to imagine what the Yankees might do with that.

What happens next? Well, you dust off, stand up and keep repeating the bright side: There is a post-

JULIAN H. GONZALEZ

Yankees manager Joe Torre and Tigers manager Jim Leyland share a laugh before the start of Game 1 of the ALDS at Yankee Stadium. Torre's team was the heavy favorite. New York went 5-2 against Detroit in the regular season.

season. The Tigers will start in New York instead of at Comerica, and they will be playing the Yankees, not the Athletics.

Finally, October in Detroit means more than falling leaves and the mathematical elimination of the Lions. Finally, the sport that defined us in the mid-'80s has returned to grace an autumn.

Tigers-Yankees. Playoff baseball.

And if the Yankees think the

World Series is their manifest destiny, well, that destiny must pass through Motown. And while the Tigers stumbled at the finish, they still won 95 games to the Yankees' 97, hit nearly as many home runs and had a far better ERA.

Besides, our team has nothing to lose. New York has about $200 million in payroll to account for.

And the Yankees don't have Murderers' Row in their lineup, they have Murderers' Section.

But New York's pitching doesn't bowl over anyone. And pitching is usually the story of these short, first-round series. The Tigers have not pitched well lately, but they pitched well early. We will see if that magic returns.

"We have the opportunity," outfielder Craig Monroe said, "to do something special."

Missed you, boys.

HOT TOPICS
Does good pitching stop good hitting? The Tigers allowed the fewest runs in the American League. The Yankees scored the most runs in the American League. Most baseball people say good pitching stops good hitting. This series will test that theory. The Yankees led the league in runs even though big hitters Gary Sheffield and Hideki Matsui missed several months with injuries. They're back.

THE X FACTOR
It's Randy Johnson. At times he can dominate. But the Big Unit is 43, and his back has been acting up. He's set to start Game 3, and that looms as the swing game of the series.

LONG SHOTS
At 12-1, the Tigers were listed as the longest shot to win the World Series. And ESPN.com, for example, had 17 experts make playoff picks, and ALL 17 went with the Yankees.

KIRTHMON F. DOZIER

The Tigers watch from the dugout in the seventh inning of an 8-4 loss to the Yankees in Game 1 of the American League Division Series. It was the Tigers' first playoff game in 19 years.

Shell-shocked

It's Glum Time as Yankees' bats overpower Robertson

By Mitch Albom

NEW YORK — It is possible, in the bazaar outside Yankee Stadium — sausages, stuffed animals, a man screaming about religion through a small amplifier, fans crushing the turnstiles to cheer the best team money can assemble — to feel, shall we say, intimidated.

But you can't play that way inside. Inside, the field is grass, the basepaths are dirt and the rules are the same: You have to get the other guys out.

Pitcher Nate Robertson, wearing glasses and looking like a college student, passed that exam for two innings.

But two innings are not enough. Come the third, the mighty Yankees began with the top of their order, and nine batters later, they had two doubles, three singles, a towering home run and a 5-0 lead.

The Tigers never stopped looking up.

"I didn't feel like I threw terrible tonight," Robertson said after the 8-4 defeat, "but ... it's just a tough lineup."

Oh, the Tigers took their swings, too. They weren't scared of Yankees starter Chien-Ming Wang. They scored three runs in the fifth inning and one in the seventh. They put a lot of runners on base. But Magglio Ordonez couldn't get runners across the plate several times, and Pudge Rodriguez did not have his typical playoff lead-the-way performance (he was 0-for-4). And the very thing Tigers fans feared most — that the weak starting pitching as of late was a habit, not a hiccup — haunted them again.

Robertson surrendered seven runs and left in the sixth.

"Overall, he didn't pitch as bad as it seemed," manager Jim Leyland said.

I'm not sure what that means. But I know it doesn't change the result. The Tigers need to turn their pitching around.

It was pretty much what the "experts" had predicted and exactly what the Tigers didn't want.

DIVISION SERIES GAME 1
Yankees 8
Tigers 4

COUNTDOWN
11

HERO
DEREK JETER
Who else? Mr. November got an early start, going 5-for-5 with three runs and a home run that put the game out of reach.

GOAT
NATE ROBERTSON
The bespectacled one gave up five runs on six straight hits in the third — ouch.

TWO CENTS
Hey, it's only one game. No panic here. It's not like the Yankees are the Royals or anything.

IN PRINT

Power-pitching rookies Justin Verlander, right, and Joel Zumaya suffocated the Yankees' big hitters. "With those kids pitching and the way we played the game," manager Jim Leyland said, "I hope at least everybody believes that we're worthy of being in the playoffs."

JULIAN H. GONZALEZ

DAMN YANKEES: Late rainout ticks off Tigers

A New York fan pokes fun of the Game 2 rain delay. But the Yankees didn't reign when Game 2 was finally played.

JULIAN H. GONZALEZ

Game 2 of the Yankees-Tigers series was postponed because of rain — and it sure did irritate the Tigers. The Tigers were upset they found out later than the Yankees did. They noticed that while they warmed up, the Yankees were nowhere to be found. Everybody knows the Yankees are a great team, but are they so great they don't even have to warm up?

"They definitely got information that I didn't have, that our team didn't have," Tigers starter Justin Verlander said.

Verlander is the main concern, of course. If he knew he was starting a game at 1:09 p.m. the next day, he would not have thrown at 9:35 p.m. the night before. And that's what he did.

The Tigers were angry. They waited and waited, and for what? Nobody seemed to know what the plan was.

Playing the Yankees is hard enough. Why must it be so hard to not play the Yankees?

BY MICHAEL ROSENBERG

PUMPED UP PEN

The Tigers' bullpen is mightier than the Yankees' swords! They're tied! They're home! So get geeked!

By Michael Rosenberg

NEW YORK — Joel Zumaya did it with a bloodshot right eye — "it's just allergies," he said.

The Yankees probably couldn't see that, but goodness, would you want to face a guy with blood in his right eye, a flame tattoo on his left forearm and a 103-m.p.h. fastball in his arsenal?

The Yankees didn't want to face this, either: a 1-1 division series tie heading back to Detroit.

In Game 2, Zumaya showed the fire. With his team clinging to a 4-3 lead and desperate for a victory, Zumaya plowed through the thickest part of the Yankees' lineup to help end a six-game losing streak.

After the game, "I called my whole entire family," Zumaya said. "They were all watching. That's how pumped I was."

My memory is foggy, but I don't recall Derek Jeter saying that after Game 1.

In the seventh and eighth innings, Zumaya struck out Jeter, Jason Giambi and Alex Rodriguez, whose combined salary of $66.7 million this year is 204 times what Zumaya makes.

As the Tigers came off the field, centerfielder Curtis Granderson playfully shouted, "That's my roomie! That's my roomie!"

I don't recall Jeter saying that in Game 1, either.

Granderson and Zumaya live together so they can, in Granderson's words, "save money."

I definitely didn't hear any Yankees use those words.

"On paper we don't match up well with those guys," closer Todd Jones said. "But we won 95 games. I think we showed today why we did win that many games."

This game looked a lot like those 95. The Tigers scored four runs, just enough. They got strong starting pitching — Justin Verlander allowed only three runs in 5⅓ innings, good numbers for a rookie against this lineup. Manager Jim Leyland made all the right moves — most notably pulling Verlander at the right time, with a 1-1 count against Robinson Cano in the sixth inning. And relievers handed the baton to one another — it went from Jamie Walker to Zumaya to Jones.

"Nobody gave us much of a chance coming up here," Jones said. "We got out of here with a split. Our work is certainly not anywhere done. ... But at least we earned some street credit today."

Not a gamble

Mr. Rogers' masterpiece gives Tigers 2-1 lead, puts Yanks on brink

By Mitch Albom

DETROIT — Kenny Rogers pushed the dirt from his coffin and rose to take the mound again. He had been buried many times before. Overpaid. Bad temper. Too old. Fades down the stretch. In Game 3, his grave was to be dug by his nibbling pitches, his crafty but slow-ball approach. Rogers hadn't beaten the Yankees in 13 years, remember? Can't you see they're the Yankees?

Yeah. We know they're the Yankees. And these are the Tigers. And before you bury a player — or his team — you better make sure they're not still squirming.

The Tigers, behind a masterful performance by the 41-year-old Rogers, beat the Yankees, 6-0, to take a 2-1 lead in this best-of-five series.

"I wanted this game as much as I ever wanted any game in my life," Rogers said after allowing five hits and striking out eight in 7⅔ innings. "A lot of people may have had us like David vs. Goliath, but I think we all felt we had a chance."

A chance? Rogers was as determined as, well, as a fighting man keeping a coffin lid from being closed.

"Maybe it comes from failing so much," Rogers said. "I'm not afraid to fail. I'm still here for a reason. I like the challenge. I know I'm fortysomething and don't have a lot of talent left ... but I do believe in myself."

ERIC SEALS
Fans stream into Comerica Park for Game 3. The CoPa had never hosted a playoff game in a city that had waited 19 years to see one.

In four innings, Rogers got batters to strike out with a runner on base, taking the steam out of any potential rally.

He whiffed Johnny Damon. He whiffed Hideki Matsui. He whiffed Bernie Williams. He whiffed Bobby Abreu.

Even more amazing, he seemed to get stronger as he went along!

"No pun intended," manager Jim Leyland said, "but I think tonight was a case where Kenny definitely got better with age."

It was a magical night in Motown. The Four Tops sang the national anthem, Al Kaline threw out the first pitch, and Ernie Harwell was back in the broadcast booth.

And the Tigers: Shut out the Yankees? Chased Randy Johnson? Mowed down Murderers' Row? One victory from the American League Championship Series?

Yep, yep, yep and yep. Let the Yankees, for once, worry about dirt being tossed on their coffin. No Tigers will die tonight.

KIRTHMON F. DOZIER

Kenny Rogers outpitched Randy Johnson in Game 3. Johnson had the most strikeouts of any left-hander in history, but he had the second-most in this game. Johnson struck out four, Rogers eight.

Jeremy Bonderman didn't need a lot of bullpen help. After not allowing a runner until the sixth inning, he left with one out in the ninth inning. He tipped, then waved his cap to the roaring, standing crowd as he left.

MANDI WRIGHT

YANKEES, GO HOME!

Tigers topple New York to win first playoff series in 22 years

By Mitch Albom

DETROIT — Yankees, go home. Tigers, go on.

Read it and blink. Read it and shake your head. Read it and ask, "Who are these guys in the Detroit uniforms?" Read it and remember just three seasons ago, when this team was in danger of sinking below oblivion.

The Detroit Tigers are in the American League Championship Series for the first time in 19 years.

This team looks nothing like the team that blew the Central Division title with a belly flop. Since the fourth inning of Game 2 at Yankee Stadium, the Tigers have been in heaven, watching their pitchers flourish, watching their hitters dominate, watching their fans delirious.

"This is the greatest feeling in the world," Jeremy Bonderman said after the 8-3 clinching victory. "It's gonna be a hell of a party. I know that."

And well earned. Bonderman pitched a perfect game for five innings, striking out Gary Sheffield, the cleanup hitter; striking out Jorge Posada, who had been hitting .500 in the series; striking out the normally unflappable Derek Jeter, getting him to chase an outside pitch.

The last out, a grounder by Robinson Cano, sent the Tigers exploding. They ran around the stadium, taking a victory lap, slapping hands with fans, even spraying them with champagne. They carried Jim Leyland off the field on their shoulders.

Could you imagine a scene like that when the season began?

In four games, one more than the minimum required, Detroit beat the heavily favored Yankees with hunger and fresh-scrubbed enthusiasm.

Detroit outscored the Yankees in this series, 22-14, and outpitched them three of four times, beating veterans Mike Mussina and Randy Johnson along the way. But the series cannot be broken down into numbers. This was a contrast in all that money can and cannot buy.

Here is what money can buy: the Yankees' magnificent roster, which has cost more than a billion dollars over the past six years and has now finished three of those seasons with a first-round exit and none of them with a World Series crown.

Here is what money cannot buy: Kenny Rogers choking up as he talked about winning his first playoff game at age 41; Leyland choking up when he talked about his players defying all odds to make the playoffs; and that happy victory lap around the stadium.

Yankees, go home.

Tigers, go on.

If this is a dream, don't you dare wake Detroit up.

DIVISION SERIES GAME 4

Tigers 8
Yankees 3

COUNTDOWN

HERO

JEREMY BONDERMAN
He didn't allow a runner until the sixth and allowed two runs and five hits in 8⅓ innings.

GOAT

JARET WRIGHT
It's hard to single one out in such a rout, but he lasted just 2⅔ innings as the Tigers jumped to a 4-0 lead.

TWO CENTS
Well, so much for the Yankees. Nice little confidence-builder before the A's, eh?

IN PRINT

Joel Zumaya and Brandon Inge share in the fans' glee after the final out. Zumaya sprayed two bottles of bubbly into the crowd. "We loved it under the radar," Zumaya screamed on the field after the game, trying unsuccessfully to match the decibel level of the fans. "We still consider ourselves the underdogs because there are a lot of people who still don't believe in us." Said Craig Monroe: "This is the best of the best, to beat the best team in baseball."

SPRAY IT! How the Tigers celebrated

Jason Grilli smiled broadly from behind a set of goofy goggles. The accompanying wipers whirred at full speed. They flicked away the stray champagne that had drenched the clubhouse at Comerica Park.

"Says it all, doesn't it?" the relief pitcher asked.

Yes, it did. The Tigers' celebration lasted long after their clinching win over the New York Yankees.

It began on the diamond, where the players hoisted manager Jim Leyland onto their shoulders as if he were Vince Lombardi. Then they went inside the clubhouse, popped a few corks, and — in an impromptu act — came back out to share the night with 43,126 of their closest friends.

Joel Zumaya, near home plate, held two bottles and sprayed both into the crowd. A thin screen was all that separated him from the eager masses.

Carlos Guillen and Magglio Ordonez hopped onto the home dugout and soaked the fans. Kenny Rogers did the same from on top of the Yankees' empty dugout. Rogers emptied a champagne bottle onto the hat of a smiling uniformed police officer in plain view of the Comerica crowd and Fox cameras.

Al Kaline, 71, danced with a cigar in hand. The players hollered and laughed.

The Tigers' celebration stopped and the clubhouse went temporarily quiet as Leyland addressed the team several minutes after the game. This is what he said:

"I know now that you know what I meant when I wrote that letter to you prior to the season. I doubt if any of you read it, and in case you didn't, go read it tonight, because I mentioned in there that we might be able to play the Yankees. We played them today, and you did pretty good."

The clubhouse erupted with cheers.

BY JON PAUL MOROSI AND JOHN LOWE

WHO's YOUR DIVISION SERIES CHAMPION?

A Comerica Park screen sports a phrase that was similar to the Tigers' season-long marketing campaign: "Who's your Tiger?" "You don't win games on paper. And they pretty much overmatched us in this series," Derek Jeter said.

JULIAN H. GONZALEZ

Brandon Inge and his teammates share a victory lap around Comerica Park with their adoring fans. The Yankees produced only three runs after Johnny Damon's three-run homer in the fourth inning of Game 2 at Yankee Stadium.

ALDS: TIGERS VS. YANKEES

Composite Box: Detroit wins series, 3-1

PITCHING SUMMARY
DETROIT

	g	cg	ip	h	r	er	bb	so	hb	wp	w	l	sv	era
Rogers	1	0	7⅔	5	0	0	2	8	1	0	1	0	0	0.00
Zumaya	2	0	2	0	0	0	3	0	0	0	0	0	0	0.00
TJones	2	0	2	1	0	0	2	0	0	0	0	0	1	0.00
Grilli	1	0	⅓	0	0	0	0	0	0	0	0	0	0	0.00
Bonderman	1	0	8⅓	5	2	2	1	4	0	0	1	0	0	2.16
JWalker	3	0	3⅔	3	2	2	1	1	0	0	1	0	0	4.91
Verlander	1	0	5⅓	7	3	3	4	5	0	0	0	0	0	5.06
Robertson	1	0	5⅓	12	7	7	0	1	2	0	1	0	0	11.12
Totals	4	0	35	33	14	14	8	24	3	0	3	1	1	3.60

NEW YORK

	g	cg	ip	h	r	er	bb	so	hb	wp	w	l	sv	era
Farnsworth	2	0	2	1	0	0	1	1	0	0	0	0	0	0.00
Rivera	1	0	1	1	0	0	1	1	0	0	0	0	0	0.00
Villone	1	0	1	1	0	0	1	1	0	0	0	0	0	0.00
Proctor	3	0	4	5	1	1	1	1	0	0	0	0	0	2.25
Bruney	3	0	2⅔	1	1	1	0	4	0	0	0	0	0	3.38
Wang	1	0	6⅓	8	3	3	1	4	0	0	1	0	0	4.05
Mussina	1	0	7	8	4	4	0	5	0	1	0	1	0	5.14
RaJohnson	1	0	5⅔	8	5	5	2	4	0	0	0	1	0	7.94
JSWright	1	0	2⅔	5	4	3	1	1	0	0	0	1	0	10.13
Lidle	1	0	1⅓	4	3	3	0	1	0	0	0	0	0	20.25
MMyers	1	0	0	1	1	0	1	0	0	0	0	0	0	INF
Totals	4	0	34	43	22	21	7	22	0	1	1	3	0	5.56

BATTING SUMMARY
DETROIT

	g	ab	r	h	2b	3b	hr	rbi	bb	so	avg
CGuillen ss	4	14	3	8	3	0	1	2	2	1	.571
Polanco 2b	4	17	3	7	1	0	0	2	1	1	.412
Casey 1b	4	17	1	6	3	0	0	4	0	1	.353
Thames dh	4	15	2	5	2	0	0	1	1	5	.333
Granderson cf	4	17	3	5	0	1	2	5	0	1	.294
MOrdonez rf	4	15	3	4	1	0	1	2	1	2	.267
IRodriguez c	4	13	3	3	1	0	0	3	2	3	.231
Monroe lf	4	16	3	3	1	0	2	3	0	3	.188
Inge 3b	4	15	1	2	0	0	0	0	0	6	.133
Totals	4	139	22	43	12	1	6	22	7	22	.309

NEW YORK

	g	ab	r	h	2b	3b	hr	rbi	bb	so	avg
Jeter ss	4	16	4	8	4	0	1	1	1	2	.500
Posada c	4	14	2	7	1	0	1	2	2	2	.500
BAbreu rf	4	15	2	5	1	0	0	4	2	2	.333
Matsui lf	4	16	1	4	1	0	0	1	0	2	.250
Damon cf	4	17	3	4	0	0	1	3	1	2	.235
Cano 2b	4	15	0	2	0	0	0	0	0	0	.133
Giambi dh	3	8	1	1	0	0	1	2	2	3	.125
Sheffield 1b	3	12	1	1	0	0	0	1	0	4	.083
ARodriguez 3b	4	14	0	1	0	0	0	0	0	4	.071
MeCabrera pr-lf	2	3	0	0	0	0	0	0	0	0	.000
APhillips 1b	1	1	0	0	0	0	0	0	0	0	.000
BWilliams dh	1	3	0	0	0	0	0	0	0	2	.000
Totals	4	134	14	33	7	0	4	14	8	24	.246

PRESS CLIPPING

Phil Rogers, Chicago Tribune: It took only a little more than 72 hours for the Tigers' powerful pitching staff to prove this wasn't the best $200 million that George Steinbrenner has ever spent. "I think we're still the best team," said Yankee Johnny Damon.

SCORE BY INNINGS

Detroit   071   074   300   —   22
New York   005   302   112   —   14

E—Grilli (1), Jeter (1), Sheffield (1), ARodriguez (1). DP—Detroit 3, New York 3. LOB—Detroit 25, New York 26. SB—Giambi (1), Granderson (1). CS—MOrdonez (1), Polanco (1), Jeter (1). S—Inge. SF—Granderson, IRodriguez. HBP—by Robertson (Giambi 2), by Rogers (ARodriguez). WP—Mussina. PB—Posada.

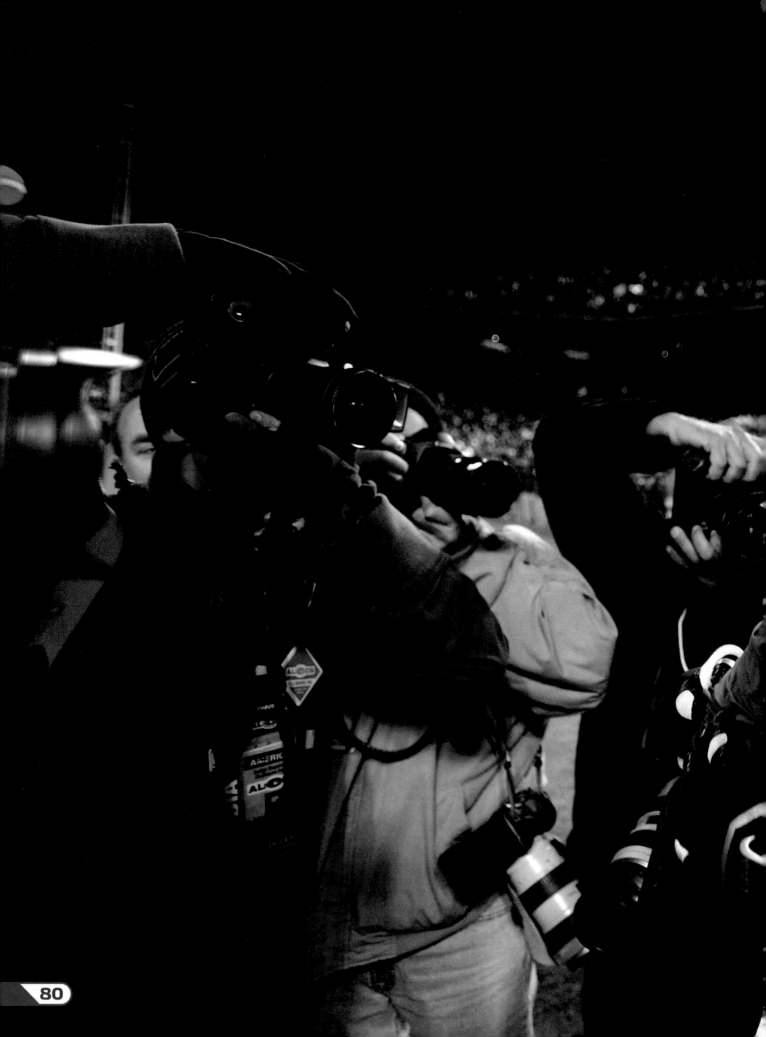

ROAR RESTORED

5 THE ALCS

Magglio Ordonez gets a hug from Jim Leyland after Ordonez's homer sent the Tigers to the Series. JULIAN H. GONZALEZ

Hot topics

What we were watching before the Tigers and A's faced off in the ALCS

WHICH TEAM IS MAGICAL?

The Tigers beat the mighty Yankees. But the Athletics ended one of the worst playoff droughts. The A's swept the Twins in three games, the first two at the Metrodome. Nine times over the span of four playoff series since 2000, the A's had lost games that would have sent them to the ALCS. So making the second round was a big deal in Oakland.

THE MATCHUPS

Most analysts predict a close series, many calling the teams even. Many think the Athletics have the advantage in hitting, defense and bench players, while the Tigers have the advantage in pitching and managing.

ROBERTSON GETS THE NOD

The Tigers announced their rotation for the Oakland series would be the same as the Yankees series. That meant Nate Robertson, Detroit's only losing pitcher in the first round, would start Game 1 opposite ace Barry Zito. Many thought Jim Leyland made the wrong decision. It would be the first of many decisions critics would question during the series.

THE BIG ACE

Zito, the guitar-playing, smooth leader of the A's, went 16-10 with a 3.83 ERA in 34 starts this season. More importantly, he shut down the Twins in Game 1 of the division playoffs, beating Twins ace Johan Santana.

THE BIG HURT

Oakland's MVP this season is designated hitter Frank Thomas, who was signed for $500,000. He started off the playoffs hot. Would his success continue?

THE BIG BEANE

A's general manager Billy Beane is the hero of sabermetricians, i.e., adorable stat-loving baseball geeks whose bible is "Moneyball." Beane challenges conventional ideas about the hit and run, bunts and stolen bases. The A's were 27th out of 30 teams in

KIRTHMON F. DOZIER

Frank Thomas led the A's with 39 homers and 114 RBIs in a comeback year. He entered the ALCS against the Tigers on a hot streak, hitting 5-for-10 with two homers in a first-round sweep of the Minnesota Twins.

sacrifice hits and 23rd in stolen bases.

THE WALKS GAP

The Tigers drew the second-fewest walks in the league this season, and the A's drew the second-most. Will the Tigers be patient enough?

LET IT FLY

Oakland is a hitter's park — the ball flies to all parts of it, and there are no huge canyons like at Comerica Park. This could be an advantage for the Tigers, who have players throughout the lineup who can get the ball in the air. The Tigers got a whopping 104 homers from the Nos. 6-9 spots in the batting order.

ONE THING IN COMMON

Detroit and Oakland do have one thing in common: lousy football teams. The Raiders (0-4) and Lions (0-5) were both winless during the baseball series.

Tigers pitchers, from left, Nate Robertson, Kenny Rogers, Jeremy Bonderman and Todd Jones warm up before the A's series. The Tigers held the Yankees scoreless for more than 20 innings, and they kept their rotation in the same order for Round 2.

WE LOVE 1972

Memories of 1972, the last time the Tigers and A's met in the playoffs:

- Jim Leyland, 27, was managing the Clinton (Iowa) Pilots to a 49-77 record as the Tigers' affiliate in the Midwest League.
- Mustaches were in.
- Dick Williams' A's — with players like Reggie Jackson, Sal Bando, Bert Campaneris, Matty Alou, Joe Rudi, Vida Blue, Blue Moon Odom, Catfish Hunter and Rollie Fingers — beat Billy Martin's Tigers in the ALCS and Sparky Anderson's Reds in the World Series.
- The Tigers had players like Al Kaline, Willie Horton, Bill Freehan, Norm Cash, Gates Brown, Dick McAuliffe, Ed Brinkman, Mickey Stanley, Jim Northrup, Mickey Lolich, Joe Coleman and John Hiller.
- Just four current Tigers were alive in '72: Kenny Rogers was 8, Todd Jones was 4, Jamie Walker and Pudge Rodriguez were 1.
- Big TV shows were "Columbo," "Rowan & Martin's Laugh-In," "Maude," "Hawaii Five-0," "Mod Squad," "The Waltons," "Sanford & Son" and the Emmy-winning "All in the Family."
- "The Godfather" won the Oscar for Best Picture, but Marlon Brando — through spokeswoman Sacheen Littlefeather — refused his Best Actor award.
- Atari released PONG.
- President Richard Nixon visited China and Russia.
- Swimmer Mark Spitz won seven gold medals at the Munich Olympics, which were marred by the deaths of 11 Israeli athletes in a terrorist attack.
- Hewlett-Packard marketed the first pocket calculator, the HP-35, for $395.

By Steve Schrader

WE HAVE, THEY HAVE

They have: Earthquakes
We have: Potholes.
They have: Mark Hamill (Luke Skywalker)
We have: U-M graduate James Earl Jones (Darth Vader)
They have: The worst team in the AFC
We have: The worst team in the NFC
They have: "Hangin' with Mr. Cooper"
We have: "Home Improvement"
They have: San Francisco, Chinatown across the bridge
We have: Windsor, Little Italy across the bridge
They have: Timothy B. Schmit (bassist for the Eagles)
We have: Glenn Frey (guitar, vocals for the Eagles)
They have: Temperatures from 45-75 degrees
We have: Temperatures from −5 to 95 degrees
They have: Al Davis and his jumpsuit
We have: William Clay Ford and inability to jump ship
They have: Receiver antics from Jerry Porter and Randy Moss
We have: Receiver antics from Mike Williams and Charles Rogers
They have: Golden State Warriors, perennial losers
We have: Wayne State Warriors, who win about as much

KIRTHMON F. DOZIER

Brandon Inge returns to a joyous dugout in the fourth inning of Game 1 after scoring the Tigers' fifth run. Inge, who had only two hits in the Yankees series, went 3-for-3 with a home run, a walk, two runs and two RBIs against Oakland.

First base-man Sean Casey walks off the field during Game 1. He sustained a small tear of the fascia muscle in his left calf and missed the rest of the series. Carlos Guillen filled in at first.

JULIAN H. GONZALEZ

WHO'S ON FIRST?

Sean Casey is known for two things. One is his immense popularity — that's why they call him The Mayor. The other is that he has the raw footspeed of a fire hydrant. But watching Casey limp to first base on a ground ball to shortstop in the sixth inning, the realization came: Not even he is that slow.

Casey pulled up with a left calf injury. He would miss the rest of the series, which meant the Tigers would have to find a new No. 3 hitter.

The good news is that the Tigers rely less on their No. 3 hitter than any team in the playoffs. Their top three home-run hitters for the season are Monroe, Marcus Thames and Brandon Inge — their No. 7, 8 and 9 hitters.

Meanwhile, Jim Leyland shifted Carlos Guillen from shortstop to first base and had to choose from among three infielders — Omar Infante, Neifi Perez or Ramon Santiago — to play shortstop.

Chris Shelton, the team's Opening Day first baseman and late-season backup, was not on the playoff roster.

Casey would return for the World Series.

One down!

Mr. October? Well, they all take turns

By Michael Rosenberg

OAKLAND, Calif. — The Tigers won another playoff game, and they did it in the usual way. By which we mean: They did it in a most unusual way.

They turned four double plays, as many as any team in League Championship Series history. They got two big hits from the last guy in the batting order. Their least ballyhooed starter outpitched the most renowned pitcher in this series.

These Tigers are not the most talented team in baseball. But they are the most balanced. All nine starters reached base in a 5-1 Game 1 victory.

If you had to pick one hitting star, you probably would go with Brandon Inge, who batted ninth. He was 2-for-15 in the playoffs entering the game.

But in Game 1, Inge hit a solo home run to give the Tigers the lead, then hit an RBI double to add to it, then scored on a Placido Polanco single. Then he singled. And then he walked. And he made great defensive plays. And then he probably sprinted back to the team hotel and put mints on all the pillows.

Oakland ace Barry Zito didn't know who would get the next hit. Zito spent the night like many residents of nearby Berkeley — high and outside. Zito was so far out of the strike zone Tuesday, even the free-swinging Tigers knew not to swing.

And while the Tigers' hitters were busy piling up runs, starting pitcher Nate Robertson was escaping jams.

The A's reached base in all five innings that Robertson pitched — and in four of those innings, they did it with no outs. Yet, he never let them score.

The closest call came in the fourth inning. The A's had runners on second and third with nobody out — and since it was still only the fourth inning, a couple of runs would have gone a long way.

But Eric Chavez came up, worked the count to 2-2 ... and struck out swinging.

And Nick Swisher came up, worked the count to 2-2 ... and struck out swinging.

And Marco Scutaro came up, worked the count to 3-2 ... and struck out looking.

The Tigers' leading gum chewer? Robertson.

Turns out he also chews up rallies.

"If they shut us down, you can't be surprised. They shut down the Yankees."

▪ A's third baseman **ERIC CHAVEZ**, on the Tigers.

CHAMPIONSHIP SERIES GAME 1

Tigers 5
Athletics ...1

COUNTDOWN

HERO
BRANDON INGE
After getting only two hits vs. the Yanks, he went 3-for-3, including a solo homer.

GOAT
BARRY ZITO
The ace lasted $3\frac{2}{3}$ innings. He's a free agent now and might have pitched his final game with the A's.

TWO CENTS
Who says the Tigers looked more patient? Last series, they waited until Game 2 to start winning. But, y'know, this might work, too.

IN PRINT

THE PLAYOFFS
GREAT ESCAPE
Jam sessions don't faze Robertson, Rodney in opener

Alexis Gomez had four RBIs in Game 2 — which set a club record for a League Championship Series game. Gomez was designated to the minors twice this season. On either of those occasions, one of the other 29 big-league clubs could have claimed him. Thankfully, no one did.

JULIAN H. GONZALEZ

Roarin' home

Leyland's lineup moves baffling, brilliant as Tigers take 2-0 lead

By Michael Rosenberg

OAKLAND, Calif. — And for his next trick, Jim Leyland will train his dog to hit a slider, then pencil him in to bat leadoff.

I don't even know if Leyland has a dog, but at this point, what's the difference? Leyland can do no wrong. Everything he touches turns into a two-run double.

The Tigers beat Oakland, 8-5, in Game 2 to pull within two wins of the World Series. And they did it thanks to lineup changes that were so bizarre, they fried baseball-geek computers around the nation.

Leyland's designated hitter was Alexis Gomez, who should not be designated to hit anything. Until Game 2, Gomez had lived 28 years and had batted 158 times in the big leagues and had one home run to show for it.

In his third at-bat against the A's, Gomez hit a home run off Esteban Loaiza.

"If I walked in there tomorrow," relief pitcher Todd Jones said, "and (the next) night I'm batting cleanup, I'd expect to get a hit."

Leyland's shortstop and No. 2 hitter

ALEXIS THE GREAT

The Tigers' Alexis Gomez nearly duplicated his season output in one ALCS game:

2006		Game 2
62	Games	1
1	HR	1
6	RBI	4

was Neifi Perez, who admitted after the game, "I'm not hitting good right now." Leyland has an odd affection for Perez. He says Perez has a lot of energy. So does Regis Philbin, and I wouldn't let him bat second, either.

Managers have all sorts of philosophies about how to put together a lineup. But generally, the No. 3 spot is reserved for the best pure hitter on the team.

But Sean Casey was injured. So Leyland went with Placido Polanco — a wonderful, underrated player, but nobody's idea of a classic No. 3 hitter.

Polanco singled in his first three at-bats. When Polanco came to bat for the fourth time, the A's intentionally walked him.

"Whatever Jim Leyland picks up and puts on paper," Casey said with a laugh, "that should be good enough for everybody."

To top off his night, Leyland had to leave his best strikeout reliever, Joel Zumaya, on the bench as the A's chipped away at Detroit's lead. Zumaya has a tight forearm. The Tigers' bullpen got six straight strikeouts anyway.

Welcome to Jim Leyland's life, circa 2006. Some of his decisions are brilliant and some aren't. But they all shine.

CHAMPIONSHIP SERIES GAME 2

Tigers 8
Athletics...5

COUNTDOWN

HERO
ALEXIS GOMEZ
The young DH made his first appearance of the playoffs on Leyland's whim and went 2-for-4, including a home run and four RBIs.

GOAT
ESTEBAN LOAIZA
The A's got their second straight bad start. Loaiza gave up seven runs on nine hits in six innings.

TWO CENTS
With three home games ahead, the pennant is within reach. Capture the flag!

IN PRINT

ANOTHER ROLLER COASTER

After Fernando Rodney struck out the side in the eighth, the roller coaster came. Todd Jones struck out the first two hitters, the next three singled to load the bases for renowned slugger Frank Thomas. Tigers fans closed their eyes. "A dramatic grand slam goes through your mind when you're sitting there," Jim Leyland said.

"I'm not going to lie about that." Said Jones: "I look up, and there's Frank Thomas as the winning run. Obviously, it's not the guy you want." But on a letter-high 1-1 fastball, Thomas swung too far underneath and flied out to centerfield. Instead of a grand slam and a tied series, the Tigers took home a 2-0 lead.

THE PLAYOFFS

SWING KINGS

Gomez's smashing postseason debut sends Athletics packing

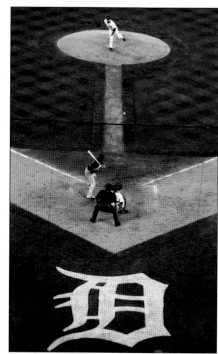

ERIC SEALS

Kenny Rogers battles the cold (it was about 40 degrees at Comerica Park) as he pitches during the seventh inning of Game 3 against the A's. Rogers shut out Oakland on two mere singles over $7^{1/3}$ innings. "Nobody could've pitched better than Kenny in these last two outings," Jim Leyland said.

SIGNS OF THE TIMES

Signs in the Comerica Park crowd after a chilly Game 3:

▪ "Game Over, Milton Bradley" for the A's outfielder.
▪ "Swisher 0-6 ALCS, Must Have Gone to 'The' Ohio State." (Yes, A's first baseman Nick Swisher is a Columbus native and Buckeyes alum.)
▪ "Kiss Your A's Good-bye."
▪ "Detroit: Home Ice Advantage."

"By the time they realize I don't have anything, the inning's over."

▪ Tigers closer **TODD JONES**, quoted in the San Diego Union-Tribune, on how he makes it through his customary one inning of work.

Left-hander Kenny Rogers reacts to the crowd after the Tigers' 3-0 victory in Game 3. Winless in nine career playoff games before this season, Rogers has won back-to-back playoff starts as a Tiger. He did not surrender a run in 15 playoff innings and struck out 14.

JULIAN H. GONZALEZ

COOL CATS

Tigers are one win from first pennant since '84

CHAMPIONSHIP SERIES
GAME 3

Tigers 3
Athletics...0

COUNTDOWN

By John Lowe

The Oakland Athletics wore the green-and-gold of America's most famous cold-weather team — the NFL's Green Bay Packers. But the Tigers were the team that looked at home in Game 3's chill. Especially their starting pitcher.

"I was trying to use the cold to my advantage," said left-hander Kenny Rogers.

It was 42 degrees at Comerica Park when Rogers threw the first pitch.

Rogers became the first Tiger to make consecutive scoreless postseason starts. As the towel-waving sellout crowd frequently chanted his first name, Rogers pitched 7⅓ innings, allowed two hits and beat the Athletics, 3-0.

Jay Payton hit into a fielder's choice to end the top of the first, and it remained Oakland's only at-bat with a runner in scoring position. The Tigers scored twice in the first off Rich Harden, and Craig Monroe homered off him in the fifth for the final run.

Fernando Rodney and Todd Jones followed Rogers with 1⅔ innings of perfect relief, and the Tigers took a 3-0 lead in the best-of-seven series.

Rogers is doing a rare thing for a major leaguer. He is vibrating with emotion on the field, and he is making it work for him. Baseball is a game of finesse and precision, and players are

MANDI WRIGHT

Brandon Inge stretches into the stands at Comerica Park to snag Mark Kotsay's foul pop-up for the first out of the game. He hung onto the ball in the crowd despite being whisked off his feet. Inge also had a hot bat in the ALCS, going 4-for-12 with three walks.

taught to play relaxed and under control.

The Tigers' defense also continued its streak of never making a misplay in the postseason that would allow a four-out inning.

Brandon Inge set the defensive tone. Early on, he made a running, lunging catch on Mark Kotsay's foul pop-up at the railing and plowed straight into the seats. Two batters into the game, Inge had landed on the dirt and on a spectator.

HERO
KENNY ROGERS
The Gambler notched his second playoff win and ran his two-game total to 15 shutout innings. Rogers notched six strikeouts, all against the prime of the order.

GOAT
FRANK THOMAS
The Big Hurt is, well, hurtin', after going 0-for-10 in the ALCS.

TWO CENTS
The Tigers deserve straight A's. So let's sweep.

IN PRINT

With Detroit waiting for a hero, Magglio Ordonez turned to Tigers clubhouse assistant Tyson Steele in the dugout. "You got the champagne on ice?" he asked Steele, before stepping onto the field in the bottom of the ninth inning. "It's over."

KIRTHMON F. DOZIER

MAGG-ICAL!

Ordonez's walk-off homer sends Tigers to Series

By Mitch Albom

DETROIT — It felt like a day of destiny. People sipped their morning coffee thinking baseball, and they dressed in layers thinking baseball, and they came to the stadium thinking baseball, baseball, baseball. It felt enlarged, this particular day in October, like something big was going to happen.

And sure enough, after a shaky start and a 3-3 score, here came the bottom of the ninth, two outs, two on — I mean, come on, is this perfect or what? — and here came your something big, folks, here came Magglio Ordonez, one of those free agents who a few years back might never have signed with the Tigers, and he smoked a 1-0 pitch so high and so far into Comerica Park's leftfield seats that he had time to watch, walk, raise a fist, then raise another fist, then run the bases pointing a new direction for this new era of Detroit baseball.

A team that three years ago suffered a classic fall is now going to the Fall Classic.

Today, the league.

Tomorrow, the world.

"When the ball went up I just went numb, tears came to my eyes," said Marcus Thames, who surged onto the field with his teammates to wait for Ordonez, one big, crazy family welcoming a brother home. "You couldn't hear anything. The fans went wild. They've been waiting such a long time. ... I feel like I'm dreaming."

Dreaming? Join the club. The World Series? The Tigers are going to the World Series?

"Not too bad, huh?" manager Jim Leyland said after the 6-3 clincher, with champagne glasses and family members all over his clubhouse office. "From 71 wins to American League

WILD FINISH

Since the advent of the wild card in 1995, eight wild-card playoff teams — including this season's Tigers — have reached the World Series. The others:

2005 Houston Astros	2004 Boston Red Sox✻	2003 Florida Marlins✻	2002 Anaheim Angels✻	2002 S.F. Giants	2000 New York Mets	1997 Florida Marlins✻

✻ Won championship

AMY LEANG

Craig Monroe scores on Ordonez's winning homer. "I had the best view of it," Monroe said. "I knew when he hit it, it was gone. The Detroit Tigers are going to the World Series. Oh, my God. We're going to the World Series."

champions?"

What a finish. What theater. How did they pull it off? It was every little thing. It was Brandon Inge beating out a ground ball, racing to second when the throw went awry and scoring two batters later. It was Curtis Granderson stretching a single into a double with smoking speed then scoring from second on Craig Monroe's double. It was Jamie Walker coming on in the seventh and ending a threat by striking out Mark Kotsay.

But it wasn't just what they did, it was what they survived. They survived an early 3-0 deficit. They survived Oakland pitcher Dan Haren's masterful control in the opening innings. They survived blown chances, none worse than the bases-loaded at-bat by Carlos Guillen in the seventh. There was one out, and Guillen did the one thing you can't do: ground into a double play to end the inning.

They survived the next half-inning, when Jason Grilli, in a meltdown moment, walked three straight batters on 12 straight pitches. Three batters? Twelve pitches? Surely, Oakland could take advantage of THAT, right?

Wrong. Wil Ledezma came in and got Marco Scutaro to foul out to end the inning. (You could hear Grilli sigh halfway to Wisconsin.)

The game stayed tied. At that point, it seemed the gods were simply horsing around, keeping it interesting, waiting until the perfect dramatic moment to bring a pennant to a pennant-starved city.

It came just before 8 o'clock, after two outs and extra innings looming, after Monroe cracked a single, and after Placido Polanco — the MVP of the series — looped another single. Then Ordonez, who hit a solo homer earlier in the game, stepped to the plate.

Ordonez took his destiny pitch over the wall, 385 feet away, and took half this state with it.

Today, the league.
Tomorrow, the world.

HOW THEY CALLED IT

FOX ON TV

Thom Brennaman: "Now Magglio Ordonez. He tied the game with a home run to leftfield in the sixth. And now Jason Kendall will come visit the mound. Dave Dombrowski, the president, getting one final stretch in, perhaps looking for divine intervention by that pose. Mike Ilitch, the owner."

Lou Piniella: "Here's where your Oakland outfield has got to cheat just a little bit. They have got to give themselves an opportunity to throw Monroe out at the plate in case of a base hit, and Payton, where he's at right now in leftfield, I don't think he has that chance."

Brennaman: "So here we go. Winning run at second base. We're in the bottom of the ninth inning. Ordonez looks at ball one inside."

Jose Mota: "It seemed to me right there, Thommy, that he was aiming for one pitch, breaking ball away somewhere."

Brennaman: "Ordonez is 0-for-2 in his career against Huston Street. In the air to leftfield! The Tigers march to the World Series! They celebrated 22 years ago today as World Series champions, and Oct. 14, 2006, the Detroit Tigers are American League champions!"

WXYT-AM (1270) ON RADIO

Dan Dickerson: "Swing and a fly ball, leftfield, it's deep, it's way back ... the Tigers are going to the World Series. Three-run, walk-off home run! Ohhh, man! Ordonez around third, he's into a mob scene at home! The Tigers have beaten the A's, 6-3, completing a four-game sweep in one of the greatest turnarounds in baseball history! The Tigers, three years after losing 119 games, are going to the World Series! Magglio Ordonez with his second home run of the game. What a sight at home plate!"

The Tigers celebrate in the clubhouse after Ordonez's big home run put them in the World Series. Backup catcher and serial goofball Vance Wilson hugged Ordonez and shouted, "Magglio's the best teammate ever!" Craig Monroe, who was mastering Spanish so he could communicate more with his Latino teammates, called Ordonez "el caballo," or "the horse," as in the one who carries a team.

ALCS: TIGERS VS. ATHLETICS

Composite Box: Detroit wins series, 4-0

PITCHING SUMMARY

DETROIT

	g	cg	ip	h	r	er	bb	so	hb	wp	w	l	sv	era
Rogers	1	0	7⅔	2	0	0	0	0	1	0	1	0	0	0.00
Robertson	1	0	5	6	0	0	3	4	0	1	0	0	0	0.00
Rodney	3	0	3⅔	1	0	0	1	4	0	0	0	0	0	0.00
TJones	3	0	3	3	0	0	1	2	0	0	0	0	2	0.00
Grilli	2	0	1	0	0	0	3	1	0	0	0	0	0	0.00
JWalker	1	0	6⅓	0	0	0	0	1	0	0	0	0	0	0.00
Ledezma	2	0	2⅔	2	1	1	1	1	0	0	1	0	0	3.38
Bonderman	1	0	6⅔	6	3	3	2	3	0	1	0	0	0	4.05
Verlander	1	0	5⅓	7	4	4	1	6	0	1	1	1	0	6.75
Zumaya	1	0	1	1	1	1	0	0	0	0	0	0	0	9.00
Totals	**4**	**0**	**27**	**29**	**9**	**9**	**14**	**28**	**1**	**2**	**4**	**0**	**2**	**3.00**

OAKLAND

	g	cg	ip	h	r	er	bb	so	hb	wp	w	l	sv	era
Gaudin	3	0	3⅔	2	0	0	3	1	0	0	0	0	0	0.00
Blanton	1	0	2	0	0	0	2	2	0	0	0	0	0	0.00
JKennedy	4	0	3⅔	2	0	0	2	2	0	1	0	0	0	0.00
Calero	3	0	2	3	0	0	1	1	0	0	0	0	0	0.00
Harden	1	0	5⅔	5	3	3	5	4	0	0	0	1	0	4.76
Haren	1	0	5	7	3	3	2	7	0	2	0	0	0	5.40
Loiaza	1	0	6	9	7	7	1	5	0	0	0	1	0	10.50
Street	2	0	3⅓	3	4	4	0	3	0	0	0	1	0	10.80
Zito	1	0	3⅔	5	5	5	3	0	0	0	0	1	0	12.27
Totals	**4**	**0**	**35**	**39**	**22**	**22**	**19**	**25**	**0**	**3**	**0**	**4**	**0**	**5.66**

BATTING SUMMARY

DETROIT

	g	ab	r	h	2b	3b	hr	rbi	bb	so	avg
Polanco 2b	4	17	2	9	1	0	0	2	2	1	.529
Infante dh	1	2	0	1	0	0	0	0	1	1	.500
AGomez dh-ph	3	9	1	4	0	0	1	4	0	2	.444
Monroe lf	4	14	5	6	2	0	1	4	3	4	.429
Granderson cf	4	15	4	5	2	0	1	2	4	2	.333
Inge 3b	4	12	3	4	1	0	1	3	3	3	.333
Casey 1b	1	3	0	1	0	0	0	0	1	0	.333
MOrdonez rf	4	17	3	4	0	0	2	6	2	2	.235
CGuillen ss-1b	4	16	1	3	1	0	0	1	2	4	.188
IRodriguez c	4	16	2	2	0	0	1	1	1	4	.125
NPerez ss	1	4	0	0	0	0	0	0	0	1	.000
RSantiago ss	3	7	0	0	0	0	0	0	1	0	.000
Thames dh-ph	2	5	1	0	0	0	0	0	0	1	.000
Totals	**4**	**137**	**22**	**39**	**7**	**0**	**7**	**22**	**19**	**25**	**.285**

OAKLAND

	g	ab	r	h	2b	3b	hr	rbi	bb	so	avg
Bradley rf	4	18	4	9	2	0	2	5	0	2	.500
Kendall c	4	17	5	5	0	0	0	0	2	2	.294
Payton lf	4	14	1	4	2	0	1	2	1	2	.286
Kotsay cf	4	16	3	4	2	0	0	0	2	3	.250
EChavez 3b	4	13	1	3	1	0	1	2	2	4	.231
DJimenez 2b	4	12	0	2	0	0	0	0	0	3	.167
Swisher 1b	4	10	0	1	0	0	0	0	5	5	.100
Scutaro ss	4	15	0	1	0	0	0	0	0	3	.067
Melhuse ph	1	1	0	0	0	0	0	0	0	1	.000
Thomas dh	4	13	0	0	0	0	0	2	0	4	.000
Kielty ph	2	2	0	0	0	0	0	0	0	0	.000
Kiger 2b	2	0	0	0	0	0	0	0	0	0	.---
Totals	**4**	**134**	**14**	**33**	**7**	**0**	**4**	**14**	**8**	**24**	**.246**

SCORE BY INNINGS

Detroit	212	733	004	—	22	
Oakland	302	101	110	—	9	
×						

E—CGuillen (1), DJimenez (2), EChavez (1). DP—Detroit 7, Oakland 4. LOB—Detroit 33, Oakland 29. SB—Granderson (1), Infante (1) S—NPerez. SF—Inge, Monroe. IBB— off Gaudin (Polanco), off JKennedy (Inge). HBP— by Rogers (Thomas).

"This is what I've dreamed about my whole career, my whole life."
— MAGGLIO ORDONEZ

ROAR RESTORED | THE ALCS 93

ROAR RESTORED

6 WORLD SERIES

WE HAVE SPIRIT: Workers hang a Tigers jersey on the Spirit of Detroit before Game 1. MANDI WRIGHT

Let's play cards!

HOT TOPICS ENTERING THE WORLD SERIES

YOU LOOK FAMILIAR

The Tigers have faced the Cardinals twice before in the World Series. The first time was in 1934, when St. Louis beat Detroit in seven games. The next time was in 1968, when the Tigers beat the Cardinals in seven games.

REUNIONS

Jeff Weaver, once the pride of the Tigers' pitching staff, now plays for the Cardinals. So does former Tigers outfielder Juan Encarnacion.

MATCHUPS

On paper, the Tigers are the much better team — they won 95 games, compared with 83 for the Cardinals, and they did it in the American League, which was much tougher than the National League. The Cardinals have the best player in this series: Albert Pujols, one of the most dominant hitters in the majors. In his career against Tigers closer Todd Jones, Pujols is 5-for-6 with two walks and three homers. And the Cards might have the best starting pitcher: Chris Carpenter, the 2005 NL Cy Young Award winner. But the Tigers are better almost everywhere else.

FRIENDSHIP NO. 1

Tigers manager Jim Leyland and Cardinals skipper Tony La Russa are extremely close — Leyland coached under La Russa years ago and worked as a scout for the Cards before taking the Tigers' job. (Leyland, perhaps aware that he has received an incredible portion of credit for a man who doesn't actually, you know, play, has said he wouldn't answer questions about his relationship with La Russa.)

FRIENDSHIP NO. 2

Placido Polanco, 31, and Pujols, 26, hail from the Dominican Republic. Polanco came up with the Cardinals in 1998. Pujols arrived in 2001. Midway through the next season, Polanco was traded to Philadelphia in the Scott Rolen deal. Polanco con-

KIRTHMON F. DOZIER

Jim Leyland, left, is one of the closest friends of Cardinals manager Tony La Russa. The two have worked together twice. Leyland was La Russa's third-base coach with the White Sox in 1982-85. Leyland was a scout for the Cardinals for six seasons before he took the Tigers' job.

siders Pujols his son's Godfather and part of the family. "I've got my best friend playing on the other side," Pujols said. "Whoever wins that ring, we are both going to be excited."

NEW ROTATION

Leyland changed the rotation. Rookie right-hander Justin Verlander would start Game 1, followed by left-handers Kenny Rogers and Nate Robertson, then right-hander Jeremy Bonderman. Leyland made the change so Rogers would pitch twice at home if necessary.

THE DH

The designated hitter is used in the American League park, but not in the National League park. That means at Busch Stadium, the Tigers' pitchers will do something they have done rarely this season — go to bat.

KIRTHMON F. DOZIER

Placido Polanco, left, says hello to his friend and ex-teammate, Albert Pujols, before Game 1. "We're playing and we're like family and we still want to beat him," Polanco said, "and I'm sure he wants to win, too." Pujols, the reigning NL MVP, entered the series batting .324 in the playoffs.

THE '68 REMATCH

What a matchup, this rematch of '68. Let's compare Motown and Beertown:

- We had Ernie Harwell. They had Jack Buck.
- We haven't won a World Series game since 1984. They haven't won a World Series game since 1987.
- They have Clydesdales. We have Mustangs, which leave less residue.
- They have celebrity fan Billy Bob Thornton, aka, "Bad Santa." We have Kid Rock, a.k.a., "American Bad Ass."
- They have the Arch, the Gateway to the West. We used to have Manny Legace's five-hole, the gateway out of the playoffs, but they have that now, too.
- They had Red Foxx. We had Red Fox (the restaurant Jimmy Hoffa was last seen at).
- They have embattled couple Ike and Tina Turner. We have embattled couple Marshall and Kim Mathers.
- We have a lousy football team. They shipped their lousy football team to Arizona and traded up to the Super Bowl-winning Rams. How'd they do that?

THEN AND NOW

The Tigers made it to the World Series for the first time since 1984. The year 1984 gave us "Thriller" and "Purple Rain." That November, a little flamethrower-to-be named Joel Zumaya was born, while a minor league pitcher with a losing record named Kenny Rogers was celebrating his 20th birthday.

1984

- Detroit population: 1.1 million
- The Bar: Lindell AC
- Double-play combo: Whitaker & Trammell
- The heat: Aurelio (Señor Smoke) Lòpez
- Detroit pop stars: Seger & Madonna
- Tigers controversy: Rowdy bleachers
- GM U.S. market share: 44%
- Highest-paid player: Jack Morris, $885,000
- Latin-born Tigers: 4
- Series box seats: $30
- How fans got them: Sleeping in line
- Stadium pizza: Domino's
- Stadium fad: the Wave
- Big hair: Willie Hernandez
- Lions: Bit the dust

2006

- Detroit population: 868,000
- The bar: Cheli's Chili
- Double-play combo: Guillen & Polanco
- The heat: Joel Zumaya
- Detroit pop stars: Kid Rock and Eminem
- Tigers controversy: Dmitri Young
- GM U.S. market share: 24.7%
- Highest-paid player: Magglio Ordonez, $16 million
- Latin-born Tigers: 10
- Series box seats: $250
- How Fans Got Them: Waiting online
- Stadium pizza: Little Caesars
- Stadium fad: Gum Time
- Big hair: Ordonez
- Lions: Still biting

Justin Verlander was moved up to be the Game 1 starter. The big matchup will be against Albert Pujols. The regular-season results were not overly encouraging. Pujols went 2-for-2, including a double, with a walk against Verlander. Meanwhile, Tony La Russa opted for Anthony Reyes, a rookie, to start Game 1, ahead of the more experienced Jason Marquis. JULIAN H. GONZALEZ

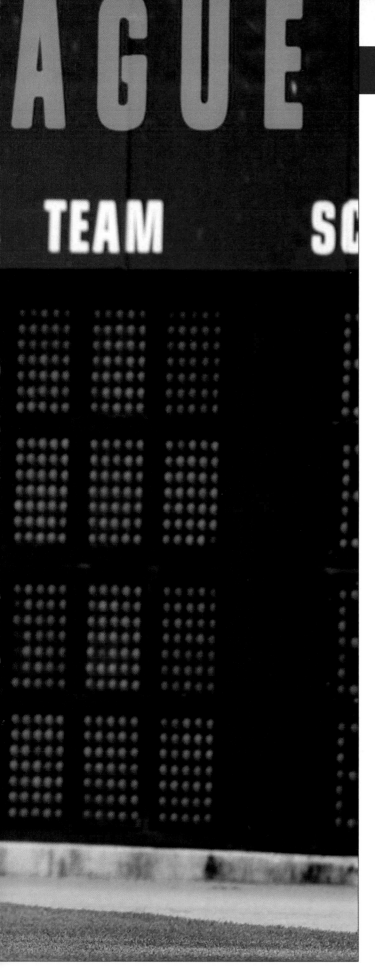

Series 101

EVERYTHING YOU EVER WANTED TO KNOW ABOUT BASEBALL'S BIGGEST STAGE

WHY DID THE TIGERS HAVE HOME-FIELD ADVANTAGE?

▌ The American League had home-field advantage because it beat the National League in the All-Star Game, 3-2. Maybe you remember the Free Press' headline the next day: TIGERS TO OPEN SERIES AT HOME. Remember. Always believe what you read in the paper (at least this paper).

WHO SHOULD TIGERS FANS THANK?

▌ Michael Young of the Texas Rangers. With Trevor Hoffman, the all-time saves leader, one strike from ending it, Young ripped a winning two-run triple.

WHICH TIGERS ALREADY HAD WORLD SERIES RINGS?

▌ Catcher Pudge Rodriguez won the title with the 2003 Florida Marlins. Left-hander Kenny Rogers won the title with the 1996 Yankees. Manager Jim Leyland and general manager Dave Dombrowski earned rings with the 1997 Marlins.

HOW MUCH MONEY DO PLAYERS GET FOR THE WORLD SERIES?

▌ Baseball creates a bonus pool for high-finishing teams based on 60% of the gate receipts from the first three games of the division series and 60% from the first four games of the later rounds. And then the players decide how to divide their stash, and whether to be good guys by including the support staff.

▌ The Chicago White Sox, for instance, won the 2005 World Series and were awarded 42 full shares, six partial shares and 22 cash awards from a pool of $14.7 million. A full share was worth $324,532.72.

▌ The runner-up Houston Astros were awarded 39 full shares, 28 partial shares and eight cash awards from a pool of $9.9 million. A full share was worth $191,985.45.

▌ If the Tigers' pool is roughly the same as the White Sox's, Joel Zumaya, Curtis Granderson and Marcus Thames will pretty much double their salaries. Dmitri Young will get a check. Troy Percival, who spent the whole season on the disabled list, won't.

TIGERS SERIES HISTORY

The Tigers haven't lost a World Series in 67 years! And have won their past three. How they have fared in 10 Series appearances:

1907
Cubs 4,
Tigers 0
1908
Cubs 4,
Tigers 1
1909
Pirates 4,
Tigers 3
1934
Cardinals 4,
Tigers 3
1935
Tigers 4,
Cubs 3
1940
Reds 4,
Tigers 3
1945
Tigers 4,
Cubs 3
1968
Tigers 4,
Cardinals 3
1984
Tigers 4,
Padres 1

Cardinals ..7
Tigers 2

COUNTDOWN

HERO
ANTHONY REYES
The rookie with 5 career victories was golden, retiring 17 straight Tigers at one point.

GOAT
JUSTIN VERLANDER
Seven runs in five innings, six of them earned? Verlander now has the worst postseason ERA (7.47) among the starters.

TWO CENTS
Somebody get the Big League Chew going right away. The Tigers will need it.

IN PRINT

FOR THE BIRDS

ERRORS, PUJOLS DOOM TIGERS

By Mitch Albom

DETROIT — This wasn't Tigers baseball. Not the brand we'd gotten used to this postseason. Home runs were surrendered. Errors were made. And the Detroit bats — swinging too often at first pitches — were all but silent.

"We didn't play well, we didn't swing the bats well, overall we didn't give a good performance," said manager Jim Leyland after the 7-2 blowout.

Justin Verlander was masterful at times, like when he struck out the side in the fourth inning. But too often he flailed. He threw balls into the dirt. He gave up a second-inning solo homer to Scott Rolen. And he made the cardinal sin against the Cardinals.

He let Albert Pujols get in his head.

In the third inning — after striking out Pujols the first time he faced him — Verlander challenged the reigning National League MVP with a runner on and a base open. You might ask why not walk him, and that would be a fair question. Verlander's first pitch was express-trained over the rightfield wall — that made it 4-1.

"It's a manager's decision to pitch him

THE TICKER

- Free Press columnist Drew Sharp: Is there any way the Tigers can revert back to their underdog status? Perhaps they can slap a "N.Y." logo on the Cardinals' cap, fooling themselves into believing that they're playing a New York team and fueling that sense of national disrespect that embodied their resolve the last time they fell behind, 1-0, in a series. What a buzz-kill Game 1 was. Detroit waited two decades for this?
- Todd Jones had some blunt words about former Tigers teammate and Cardinals Game 2 starter Jeff Weaver. "There's no love lost here that he's gone," Jones said. Weaver took the high road: "Todd Jones is one of the nicest guys I've ever run across. If he's got unkind words for me, I don't know what they're stemming from."
- Former Tigers broadcaster Ernie Harwell, 88, worked an inning of radio for the Tigers. Fans even got to hear "Long gone!" on Scott Rolen's home run call.

or walk him," Leyland said. "I take the bullet there."

Verlander disagreed: "I made a little bit of a mistake that maybe the ninth hitter wouldn't have hit. But it was Albert Pujols ... and he made it hurt."

The Tigers made three errors, two in the sixth inning. Verlander threw the ball away, and Brandon Inge bobbled a ball and threw it away.

"We didn't play well, we didn't swing the bats well, overall we didn't give a good performance."

■ Manager **JIM LEYLAND**, on the Tigers' Game 1 loss.

KIRTHMON F. DOZIER

GAME 1

Cardinals 7
Tigers 2

ST. LOUIS	ab	r	h	rbi	bb	so	avg.
Eckstein ss	5	0	0	0	0	1	.000
Duncan dh	4	1	1	1	0	2	.250
b-PrWilson ph-dh	1	0	0	0	0	1	.000
Pujols 1b	3	2	1	2	1	1	.333
Edmonds cf	4	1	2	1	0	2	.500
Rolen 3b	4	2	2	1	0	1	.500
JEncarnacion rf	3	0	0	1	1	0	.000
Belliard 2b	4	0	0	0	0	1	.000
YMolina c	4	1	1	0	0	1	.250
Taguchi lf	4	0	1	0	0	0	.250
Totals	36	7	8	6	2	10	

DETROIT	ab	r	h	rbi	bb	so	avg.
Granderson cf	4	0	0	0	0	0	.000
Monroe lf	4	2	2	1	0	0	.500
Polanco 2b	4	0	0	0	0	0	.000
MOrdonez rf	3	0	0	0	1	1	.000
CGuillen 1b	4	0	2	1	0	1	.500
IRodriguez c	4	0	0	0	0	0	.000
Casey dh	3	0	0	0	0	1	.000
Inge 3b	3	0	0	0	0	1	.000
RSantiago ss	2	0	0	0	0	1	.000
a-Thames ph	1	0	0	0	0	0	.000
NPerez ss	0	0	0	0	0	0	---
Totals	32	2	4	2	1	5	

St. Louis .....013 003 000 — 7 8 2
Detroit ....100 000 001 — 2 4 3

a-popped out for Santiago in the 8th. b-struck out for Duncan in the 9th.

E: Rolen (1), JEncarnacion (1), Inge 2 (2), Verlander (1). **LOB:** St. Louis 4, Detroit 4. **2B:** Duncan (1), Rolen (1), Monroe (1). **HR:** Monroe (1), off Reyes; Pujols (1), off Verlander; Rolen (1), off Verlander. **RBI:** Duncan (1), Pujols 2 (2), Edmonds (1), Rolen (1), JEncarnacion (1), Monroe (1), CGuillen (1).

Runners left in scoring position: St. Louis 2 (PrWilson, Taguchi); Detroit 2 (IRodriguez 2).

Runners moved up: Taguchi.

St. Louis	ip	h	r	er	bb	so	np	era
Reyes (W, 1-0)	8	4	2	2	1	4	92	2.25
Looper	1	0	0	0	0	1	22	0.00
Detroit	ip	h	r	er	bb	so	np	era
Verlander (L, 0-1)	5	6	7	6	2	8	96	10.80
Grilli	1	0	0	0	0	1	11	0.00
Rodney	1	0	0	0	0	1	12	0.00
Ledezma	1	1	0	0	0	0	15	0.00
TJones	²⁄₃	1	0	0	0	0	8	0.00
JWalker	¹⁄₃	0	0	0	0	1	7	0.00

Reyes pitched to 1 batter in the 9th, Verlander pitched to 3 batters in the 6th. **Inherited runners-scored:** Grilli 2-2, JWalker 1-0. **WP:** JWalker. **Umpires:** Home, Randy Marsh; 1b, Alfonso Marquez; 2b, Wally Bell; 3b, Mike Winters; Left, John Hirschbeck; Right, Tim McClelland. **T:** 2:54. **A:** 42,479 (41,070).

Jim Edmonds scores as Tigers catcher Pudge Rodriguez stretches for a wild throw by third baseman Brandon Inge in the sixth inning. Inge bobbled ex-Tiger Juan Encarnacion's grounder before the throw. The Tigers made three errors in Game 1, two by Inge.

It was that kind of game.

And thanks to the impatience — and perhaps rust — of the Tigers' batters, Cardinals rookie Anthony Reyes was still out there in the ninth inning and had thrown 90 pitches. His performance will go down as one of the most unlikely in World Series history.

"I hope my next three pitch as well as my first one," Cardinals manager Tony La Russa said.

Hey, Tigers. I know all the experts were picking you to win this thing, but don't feel an obligation to help balance the odds.

It was a great scene down at the ballpark, a great atmosphere, a great sight of Bob Seger singing "America the Beautiful" and Ernie Harwell doffing his cap on the pitcher's mound.

But great feelings don't win ballgames, great pitching and hitting do. The Cardinals got plenty in each category, and it was enough to slap the Tigers out of the dreamy euphoria we have all been lounging in and remind them that four more victories are required before they have happy dreams all winter.

Kenny Rogers reacts after getting an out in Game 2. Rogers and one other pitcher in history — N.Y. Giants right-hander Christy Mathewson in 1905 — have three scoreless starts in the same postseason.
JULIAN H. GONZALEZ

MR. FREEZE

KEN YOU BELIEVE IT? ROGERS CHILLS CARDS TO TIE SERIES AT 1

CHAMPIONSHIP SERIES GAME 2

Tigers 3
Cardinals...1

COUNTDOWN

3

HERO
KENNY ROGERS
He allowed just two hits in eight innings and has pitched 23 consecutive scoreless postseason innings, sixth all-time.

GOAT
JEFF WEAVER
The ex-Tiger wasn't bad, but just wasn't as good as the other guy.

TWO CENTS
Any gambler knows there's no such thing as a sure bet, right? Well, meet Kenny Rogers.

IN PRINT

By Mitch Albom

DETROIT — On a night when the weather said it's time to stop playing baseball, Kenny Rogers took the mound and said no, we play on, we play like Game 1 never happened, we play like this magical Detroit year is still, well, magical. Rogers lifted his teammates' chins, said, "Watch the old man do it," went out there and hurled a masterpiece.

He did it by allowing no runs and two hits in eight innings. He did it by shutting down the creature from another planet, Albert Pujols. He did it by striking out the cleanup hitter, Scott Rolen, to end a frame, and by striking out the No. 5 hitter, Juan Encarnacion, and No. 6 hitter, Jim Edmonds, to start frames. He did it by making four sharp fielding plays at the mound.

He did it despite dangerously thin run support for much of the night. The Tigers scored two runs in the first and one in the fifth, leaving more men stranded than the pilot of "Lost."

But half a run might have been enough for Rogers. He now has won three times in the postseason, all of them shutout performances.

This from a guy who had never won a playoff game.

"When it came to pressure, I used to be the poster boy for failure," Rogers said after the 3-1 victory tied the Series at 1.

It was Appreciate Your Elders Night at Comerica Park. Anita Baker sang the national anthem. Sparky Anderson, dapper in a gray sports coat and lime turtleneck, threw out the ceremonial first pitch. Alan Trammell brought the ball to the mound to a thunderous ovation.

And the Tigers' bats responded quickly, too. In the first inning, Craig Monroe smacked a Jeff Weaver pitch a good 420 feet to left-center, making it two home runs in two swings (he hit one late in Game 1). Carlos Guillen smacked a double to score Magglio Ordonez and, just like that, it was 2-0.

That was all the scoring for more than an hour.

The Tigers loaded the bases in the fourth inning. Their 1-2-3 hitters went 1-2-3, a strikeout, a pop-up and a groundout. But everything was fine with Rogers there.

A moment here for something TV made into a big controversy. After the first inning, Fox showed what seemed to be a dark substance on Rogers' left hand, his pitching hand. When he came out for the second inning, it was gone. Manager Jim Leyland said: "They made Kenny wash his hands, and he was pretty clean the rest of the way." Rogers said it was "a clump of dirt and rosin." The umpire supervisor, Steve Palermo, dismissed it as exactly that — which didn't stop the media corps from acting as if they'd discovered a weapon of mass destruction.

Well, it is the World Series. Even the little is BIG. But let's face it. Rogers could have had a Slinky attached to the ball the way he was pitching. "I think he's on a mission," Leyland said.

Mission, once again, accomplished.

Tigers 3
Cardinals 1

ST. LOUIS	ab	r	h	rbi	bb	so	avg.
Eckstein ss	4	0	0	0	0	0	.000
Spiezio dh	3	0	0	0	1	1	.000
Pujols 1b	3	0	0	0	1	0	.167
Rolen 3b	4	1	2	0	0	1	.500
JEncarnacion rf	4	0	0	0	0	1	.000
Edmonds cf	3	0	1	1	1	1	.429
PrWilson lf	3	0	0	0	0	0	.000
YMolina c	4	0	1	0	0	0	.250
Miles 2b	3	0	0	0	0	1	.000
Totals	**31**	**1**	**4**	**1**	**3**	**5**	

DETROIT	ab	r	h	rbi	bb	so	avg.
Granderson cf	5	0	0	0	0	2	.000
Monroe lf	3	1	1	1	1	1	.429
Polanco 2b	3	0	0	0	0	1	.000
MOrdonez rf	4	1	2	0	0	0	.286
CGuillen 1b	3	1	3	1	1	0	.714
IRodriguez c	4	0	0	0	0	1	.000
Casey dh	3	0	1	1	0	0	.167
Inge 3b	4	0	2	0	0	2	.286
RSantiago ss	3	0	1	0	0	1	.200
Totals	**32**	**3**	**10**	**3**	**2**	**8**	

St. Louis ....000 000 001 — 1 4 1
Detroit ....200 010 00x — 3 10 1

E: Pujols (1), TJones (1). **LOB:** St. Louis 7, Detroit 10. **2B:** Edmonds (1), CGuillen (1). **3B:** CGuillen (1). **HR:** Monroe (2), off JfWeaver. **RBI:** Edmonds (2), Monroe (2), CGuillen (2), Casey (1). **S:** RSantiago. **GIDP:** Eckstein, Granderson, IRodriguez.

Runners left in scoring position: St. Louis 3 (JEncarnacion, YMolina 2); Detroit 4 (Polanco 2, MOrdonez 2).

DP: St. Louis 2 (Miles, Eckstein and Pujols), (Rolen, Miles and Pujols); Detroit 1 (Polanco, RSantiago and CGuillen).

St. Louis	ip	h	r	er	bb	so	np	era
JfWeaver (L 0-1)	5	9	3	3	1	5	85	5.40
TJohnson	²/₃	0	0	0	1	9	0.00	
Kinney	¹/₃	0	0	0	1	0	8	0.00
Flores	1	1	0	0	0	12	0.00	
Thompson	²/₃	0	0	0	1	8	0.00	
Wainwright	¹/₃	0	0	0	1	5	0.00	
Detroit	ip	h	r	er	bb	so	np	era
Rogers (W 1-0)	8	2	0	0	3	5	99	0.00
TJones S, 1	1	2	1	0	0	15	0.00	

HBP: by TJones (PrWilson), by Kinney (Polanco), by JfWeaver (Casey).

Umpires: Home, Alfonso Marquez; 1b, Wally Bell; 2b, Mike Winters; 3b, John Hirschbeck; Left, Tim McClelland; Right, Randy Marsh.
T: 2:55. **A:** 42,533 (41,070).

KIRTHMON F. DOZIER

Kenny Rogers pitches in the first inning of Game 2. Cameras showed a substance on Rogers' hand, and a national controversy emerged. But after the substance was washed off, Rogers pitched seven more scoreless innings.

Rogers cheated, but is it really so bad?

By Michael Rosenberg

This should be obvious to everybody by now, but Kenny Rogers cheated. He put a gob of pine tar on his hand so he could grip the ball better in his three postseason starts. There are plenty of other questions — whether it SHOULD be cheating; if it's a big deal, since many pitchers have done this for years, and whether Cardinals manager Tony La Russa should have gotten Rogers kicked out of the game.

Baseball has degrees of cheating. A little pine tar in cold weather is not as bad as scuffing the ball, which is not as bad as throwing a spitball, which is not as bad as using a video camera in centerfield to steal signs, which is not as bad as using steroids to gain 30 pounds of muscle.

La Russa probably made the pragmatic decision. After all, Tigers skipper Jim Leyland worked for the Cardinals the last few years; he probably knows which Cardinals are cheating a little, too.

Rogers' mistake, baseball people say privately, was getting caught. If anything, he seems to be an inexperienced cheater, at least when it comes to pine tar.

Remember, he spent much of his career in warm-weather Texas. That's probably why he had the pine tar on his hand instead of his glove, where nobody would have noticed it.

This off-season, MLB should relax its rules on gripping the ball in cold weather a little bit, then actually enforce them. Otherwise, it looks like cheating is OK with everybody.

Foul play? THE ROGERS DEBATE

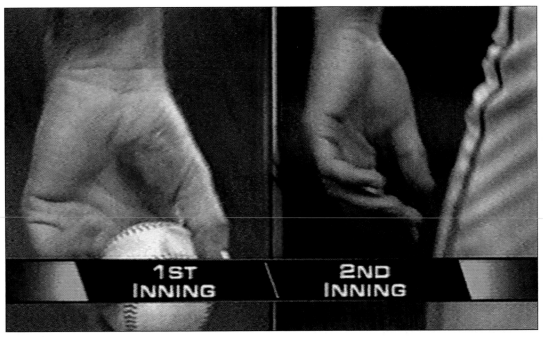

1ST INNING | 2ND INNING

FOX TV SCREEN CAPTURE

Fox television cameras detected a strange substance on Kenny Rogers' pitching hand in the first inning. Conspiracy theories abounded. Was it pine tar? The Cardinals asked that Rogers wash the substance off, and he did before the second inning.

Kenny Rogers' Smudgegate controversy began when Fox cameras captured a yellow-brown splotch on the palm of Rogers' throwing hand during Game 2. Rogers explained that the substance, which he said he wiped away after the first inning, was "a big clump of dirt." ESPN repeatedly has displayed photos showing that Rogers had a similar spot on his hand during earlier postseason starts. The reactions:

■ **Rogers:** "I rub up baseballs all the time," he said. "I rub balls before I pitch in the bullpen. I'm not going to stop doing it. My routine is my routine. Nobody likes to throw a brand new baseball. I like the dirt on it, mud on it, spit, rosin, whatever you want to talk about. I use all that stuff to get the ball to where you can feel it."

THE RULES

■ Baseball prohibits pitchers from having foreign substances on their bodies while throwing during the game. Dirt and mud from the field, or rosin from the bag that rests on the nape of the mound, would be legal, because they are part of the playing field. Spit is illegal.

■ **Cardinals manager Tony La Russa:** "Didn't look like dirt." And, "I said" to the umpire "let's get it fixed. If it gets fixed, let's play the game. ... If he didn't get rid of it, I would have challenged."

■ **Tigers closer Todd Jones** went so far as to admit that he occasionally used pine tar to help him grip the ball while pitching for the Colorado Rockies in 2002 and 2003. Jones characterized pine tar as a substance that did not affect the ball's path, but simply helped him grip the ball while pitching at high altitudes. He said that reduced the chance the batter would be hit by a pitch. "This is not brand-new, guys," Jones told reporters. "Seriously. Hitters use it. Catchers use it on their shin guards. Infielders have it on their gloves. It's an accepted thing."

■ **Hal McRae, the St. Louis hitting coach**, told USA Today that Rogers had been blatant in his disregard for the rules. "What was so strange about it was how obvious it was, in the World Series," McRae said. "It's a shame a guy would cheat in a World Series game. It hurts the integrity of the game."

VERDICT

WHY KENNY'S INNOCENT

■ Cleaned up after the first and threw seven innings of one-hit ball.
■ It's no secret pitchers might use a little something — such as pine tar — to help their grip. The crime? It's like jaywalking.
■ The umpires didn't eject him, right?
■ Tony La Russa didn't blow a gasket. The Cardinals didn't really chirp.

WHY KENNY'S GUILTY

■ Same smudge appears all during the playoffs.
■ He's 41, he had a career 8.85 playoff ERA and now he has thrown 23 straight scoreless innings — something has to be up.
■ Rules are rules. If it's on the palm, it'll find its way to the fingers and ball.
■ Baseball folks rarely rat out their own, so read between the lines.

CHAMPIONSHIP
SERIES
GAME 3

Cardinals ..5
Tigers 0

COUNTDOWN

HERO
**CHRIS
CARPENTER**
He looked every
bit the ace for
the Cardinals,
shutting down
the Tigers for
eight innings on
three hits.

GOAT
**TIGERS
HITTERS**
Or lack thereof.
The top six in
the order com-
bined for an 0-
for-20 night.

TWO CENTS
Next game is
pretty much
must-win, isn't
it? Aw, we said
the same thing
in '68, so what
do we know?

IN PRINT

BIRD BATH

TIGERS FALL BEHIND, 2-1, MUST START HITTING – OR ELSE

By Michael Rosenberg

ST. LOUIS — Enough, for a moment, about the pine tar or whatever that was on Kenny Rogers' left palm. The biggest mystery of this World Series is who stole the Tigers' bats.

It's true that, with the World Series shifting to the National League ballpark, the Tigers have to let their pitchers hit. But that doesn't mean they all have to hit like pitchers.

The Cardinals beat the Tigers, 5-0, in Game 3 of the World Series. If the rules were changed and every Tigers hit counted for a run, the Tigers still would have lost, 5-3.

The Cardinals now have a 2-1 series lead, and if you want the story of Game 4, here it is:

"If we don't swing the bats better, they'll go up, 3-1," Tigers manager Jim Leyland said. "That's as simple as it is."

Curtis Granderson is hitless for the World Series. Placido Polanco is hitless for the World Series. Pudge Rodriguez is hitless for the World Series. Those are the Tigers' Nos. 1, 3 and 6 hitters. And because the game was in St. Louis, starting pitcher Nate

> ## "If we don't swing the bats better, they'll go up, 3-1. That's as simple as it is."
>
> ■ Skipper **JIM LEYLAND**, on the Tigers' lack of production in Game 3 of the World Series.

Tigers catcher Pudge Rodriguez writhes in pain after taking a foul ball in the eighth inning. Rodriguez is 0-for-11 in the World Series and is hitless in his past six postseason games. "He has pressed to the point where it has gotten the best of him," Jim Leyland said. MANDI WRIGHT

Robertson batted ninth. One, three, six, nine ... let's swing at everything and get home in time!

Everything that seemed so right is going terribly wrong.

Leyland's decisions (starting rookie Justin Verlander in Game 1, batting Polanco third) are backfiring. And Joel Zumaya's arm, which has saved so many runs for the Tigers this season, cost them two in Game 3.

In his first appearance in two weeks, Zumaya got into trouble with a pair of walks to open the seventh inning. Albert Pujols was up.

Zumaya somehow got Pujols to bounce back to the mound. He should have thrown to second base to start a double play. Surprisingly, he turned toward third base instead. And more surprisingly, he threw to leftfield.

Two Cardinals scored. St. Louis led, 4-0, and the way the Tigers were swinging, that felt like a four-touchdown lead over the Lions.

Meanwhile, starter Chris Carpenter was brilliant. And here is where the Tigers' biggest weakness came into play: When a top pitcher has his best stuff, a team needs to be patient, make the most out of every at-bat and run up the starter's pitch count so that another pitcher must replace him.

These Tigers can't do that. It's not in their DNA. There are guys on this roster who haven't taken a pitch since Little League. For much of the night, Carpenter was on a 10-pitch-inning pace.

The Tigers have gotten this far with their free-swinging ways, and they might yet win the World Series. But if they lose two more games, then it probably will be because their biggest flaw caught up to them.

JULIAN H. GONZALEZ

Brandon Inge throws his helmet after hitting into a double play to end the eighth inning of Game 3. Manager Jim Leyland switched up his lineup for Game 4, dropping Placido Polanco down to No. 7. "I think every once in a while you post the lineup," Leyland said, "and it looks different and ... you hope just something like that maybe shakes things up."

"He gave it right to me and I messed it up."

■ JOEL ZUMAYA, on his throwing mistake off an Albert Pujols ground ball to the mound.

WHERE'S THE OFFENSE?

The Tigers averaged just 1.6 runs in the first three games against the Cardinals. They averaged 5.5 runs per game in the first two rounds of the playoffs. The main culprits against the Cards:

FOR THE SERIES
■ Curtis Granderson 0-for-13
■ Pudge Rodriguez 0-for-11
■ Placido Polanco 0-for-10

IN GAME 3
■ Granderson, Polanco, Rodriguez, Craig Monroe, Carlos Guillen and Magglio Ordonez were 0-for-20.

TIGERS LOVE WRESTLING

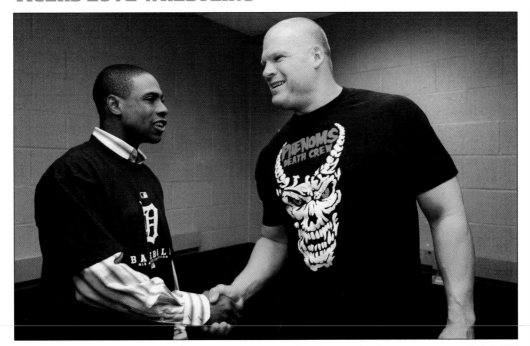

Courtesy: WWE

Curtis Granderson shakes — but doesn't wrestle with — Kane, listed at 7-feet, 325 pounds with a signature move called "Chokeslam." Granderson said he can't wait for Wrestlemania 23 at Ford Field on April 1, the day before the Tigers' 2007 opener.

Before Game 3, a few Tigers got to chat with their big heroes.

The WWE professional wrestling league was in St. Louis to tape its weekly "SmackDown" show. And a few of the Tigers are big fans. Curtis Granderson, Sean Casey and Joel Zumaya zipped over to the Scottrade Center in downtown St. Louis to chat with wrestlers such as Batista, Kane and Mr. Kennedy.

"It was awesome. I got to meet so many of the guys that I grew up watching," Granderson told WWE.com. "Some of my favorites were the Million Dollar Man and Rey Mysterio. If we ever got to add a WWE superstar to our roster, it would be Rey. He is so fast. He'd make a great pinch-runner."

Casey, 32, has been to several WWE shows. Zumaya, 21, wrestled with his brother growing up.

Granderson, 25, started watching pro wrestling when he was about 8. "We'd record pay-per-views for my grandma," he said.

Later in Game 3, the chatterbox Casey talked on the field with Cardinals shortstop David Eckstein about wrestling as Eckstein was on first.

SHAWN WINDSOR

FANS BASH ROGERS

Signs around Busch Stadium in St. Louis made fun of Kenny Rogers' Smudgegate:

- "The Detroit Cheetahs."
- "Got Dirt? Keep it clean!"
- "The Gambler has a dirty hand."
- "The Cardinals will beat the tar out of the Tigers."
- A Hard Rock Café kiosk advertised $6 Rogers brats (dirt optional). Another kiosk sold bags of makeshift brown stick-on patches. An accompanying sign read, "Buy your pine tar here: $3."
- A local radio station used brown stage makeup to put scuff marks resembling pine tar on people's palms.

KIRTHMON F. DOZIER

In Game 3 at Busch Stadium, Cardinals fans teed off on Kenny Rogers with creative signs. The topic dominated the off day between Games 2 and 3. "We beat the Yankees, and they want to fire Joe Torre," the Tigers' Brandon Inge said. "We beat Oakland and they want to fire their manager. Everyone wants to discredit everything we do."

GAME 3

Cardinals 5
Tigers 0

DETROIT	ab	r	h	rbi	bb	so	avg.
Granderson cf	4	0	0	0	0	2	.000
Monroe lf	4	0	0	0	0	1	.273
Polanco 2b	3	0	0	0	0	0	.000
MOrdonez rf	3	0	0	0	0	0	.200
CGuillen ss	3	0	0	0	0	1	.500
IRodriguez c	3	0	0	0	0	1	.000
Casey 1b	3	0	2	0	0	0	.333
Inge 3b	3	0	1	0	0	1	.300
Rodney p	0	0	0	0	0	0	---
Miner p	0	0	0	0	0	0	---
Robertson p	0	0	0	0	0	0	---
a-AGomez ph	1	0	0	0	0	0	.000
Ledezma p	0	0	0	0	0	0	---
Zumaya p	0	0	0	0	0	0	---
Grilli p	0	0	0	0	0	0	---
NPerez 3b	0	0	0	0	0	0	---
b-Infante ph	1	0	0	0	0	0	.000
Totals	**28**	**0**	**3**	**0**	**0**	**6**	

ST. LOUIS	ab	r	h	rbi	bb	so	avg.
Eckstein ss	4	1	2	0	1	0	.154
PrWilson lf	3	1	1	0	2	1	.143
Pujols 1b	4	1	1	0	0	0	.200
Rolen 3b	4	1	1	0	1	1	.417
Belliard 2b	4	0	0	0	0	1	.000
Edmonds cf	2	0	1	2	2	1	.444
YMolina c	3	0	1	0	1	0	.273
Taguchi rf	3	1	0	0	1	1	.143
Carpenter p	3	0	0	0	0	0	.000
Looper p	0	0	0	0	0	0	---
Totals	**30**	**5**	**7**	**2**	**8**	**5**	

Detroit........000 000 000 — 0 3 1
St. Louis .....000 200 21x — 5 7 0

a-grounded out for Robertson in the 6th. b-grounded out for Perez in the 9th.

E: Zumaya (1). **LOB:** Detroit 2, St. Louis 11.
2B: Pujols (1), Edmonds (2), YMolina (1).
RBI: Edmonds 2 (4). **S:** Robertson, Carpenter.
GIDP: Inge, Rolen.

Runners left in scoring position: Detroit 1 (Granderson); St. Louis 5 (Belliard, YMolina, Carpenter 3).

Runners moved up: Rolen.

DP: Detroit 1 (NPerez and Casey); St. Louis 1 (Rolen, Belliard and Pujols).

Detroit	ip	h	r	er	bb	so	np	era
Robertson (L, 0-1)	5	5	2	2	3	3	93	3.60
Ledezma	⅓	1	0	0	0	1	10	0.00
Zumaya	1	0	2	0	2	1	24	0.00
Grilli	⅔	0	0	0	1	0	11	0.00
Rodney	⅓	1	1	1	2	0	17	6.75
Miner	⅔	0	0	0	0	0	8	0.00

St. Louis	ip	h	r	er	bb	so	np	era
Carpenter (W, 1-0)	8	3	0	0	0	6	82	0.00
Looper	1	0	0	0	0	0	11	0.00

Inherited runners-scored: Miner 3-1, Zumaya 1-0, Grilli 1-0.
IBB: off Grilli (Edmonds) 1, off Robertson (YMolina) 1. **HBP:** by Miner (Pujols). **WP:** Miner, Carpenter.
Umpires: Home, Wally Bell; 1b, Mike Winters; 2b, John Hirschbeck; 3b, Tim McClelland; Left, Randy Marsh; Right, Alfonso Marquez.
T: 3:03. **A:** 46,513 (43,975).

Curtis Granderson slips and falls on the slick grass while trying to make the catch on a David Eckstein fly ball. The ball sailed over him to the wall for a double. It reminded many of the 1968 Series between the Tigers and Cardinals, when St. Louis centerfielder Curt Flood misjudged Jim Northrup's two-run triple in Game 7. ERIC SEALS

SLIPPING AWAY

TIGERS BLOW A 3-0 LEAD, FALL INTO A 3-1 HOLE

By Mitch Albom

ST. LOUIS — This is what the brink looks like. It looks like a ball flying over Curtis Granderson's head. As he chases it running backward his legs go out, like someone pulled the tablecloth, a sure out has turned into a double. His uniform is wet. His face is red.

This is what the brink looks like. A simple bunt, coming Fernando Rodney's way, and Rodney runs off the mound, and he picks it up, he throws to first base, a simple out — isn't it simple? — but he throws too high, it soars over the fielder's head, a run comes in, the game is tied. He is angry. His face is red.

This is what the brink looks like. A two-out line shot that comes flying Craig Monroe's way, and he digs and he leaps and the ball hits his glove — and then bounces off the webbing. He falls to the ground. The winning run scores. He is wet. The whole stadium is red.

This is what the brink looks like — because the Tigers are on it now. A game they had (with a 3-0 lead) and gave away. A slip. A bad throw. A wild pitch. Another error on another Tigers pitcher on a staff that in four games has committed more errors than any pitching staff in World Series history.

"Basically, they've played good enough

CHAMPIONSHIP
SERIES
GAME 4
Cardinals ..5
Tigers 4

COUNTDOWN

HERO
DAVID ECKSTEIN
His fourth hit and third double of the night was the winner in the eighth.

GOAT
THE BULLPEN
No wonder Bonderman didn't want to come out. Rodney committed an error. Zumaya was wild. And both gave up go-ahead runs on two-out hits.

TWO CENTS
Down 3-1? Forget '84. If we're gonna party now, it'll have to be like '68.

IN PRINT

ERIC SEALS

Placido Polanco, covering first, can't get to a ball thrown by pitcher Fernando Rodney. Rodney took a bunt from So Taguchi, an easy play, a sure out, but Rodney threw it over the head of Polanco. David Eckstein came around to score.

Cardinals 5
Tigers 4

DETROIT	ab	r	h	rbi	bb	so	avg.
Granderson cf	5	1	1	0	0	2	.056
Monroe lf	5	0	0	0	0	1	.188
CGuillen ss	3	1	1	0	2	1	.462
MOrdonez rf	5	0	0	0	0	2	.133
Casey 1b	4	1	3	2	0	0	.462
IRodriguez c	4	1	3	1	0	0	.200
Polanco 2b	4	0	0	0	0	0	.000
Inge 3b	3	0	2	1	1	0	.385
Bonderman p	2	0	0	0	0	1	.000
Rodney p	0	0	0	0	0	0	---
c-AGomez ph	1	0	0	0	0	1	.000
Zumaya p	0	0	0	0	0	0	---
Totals	36	4	10	4	3	8	

ST. LOUIS	ab	r	h	rbi	bb	so	avg.
Eckstein ss	5	1	4	2	0	0	.333
Duncan rf	2	0	0	0	1	0	.167
b-Taguchi ph-rf-lf	1	1	0	0	0	0	.125
Pujols 1b	2	0	0	0	2	1	.167
Edmonds cf	4	0	0	0	0	3	.308
Rolen 3b	4	1	2	0	0	1	.438
PrWilson lf	3	0	1	1	0	0	.200
Wainwright p	0	0	0	0	0	0	---
YMolina c	2	0	1	1	2	0	.308
Miles 2b	3	2	1	0	1	1	.167
Suppan p	2	0	0	0	0	1	.000
a-Rodriguez ph	1	0	0	0	0	1	.000
Kinney p	0	0	0	0	0	0	---
TJohnson p	0	0	0	0	0	0	---
Looper p	0	0	0	0	0	0	---
JEncarnacion rf	1	0	0	0	0	1	.000
Totals	30	5	9	4	6	9	

```
Detroit ........012 000 010 — 4 10 1
St. Louis .....001 100 21x — 5  9 0
```

a-struck out for Suppan in the 6th. b-safe on sacrifice plus error for Duncan in the 7th. c-struck out for Rodney in the 8th.

E: Rodney (1). **LOB:** Detroit 9, St. Louis 9. **2B:** Granderson (1), IRodriguez (1), Inge (1), Eckstein 3 (3), Rolen 2 (3), YMolina (2). **HR:** Casey (1), off Suppan. **RBI:** Casey 2 (3), IRodriguez (1), Inge (1), Eckstein 2 (2), PrWilson (1), YMolina (1). **SB:** CGuillen (1), Miles (1). **S:** Bonderman, Taguchi, PrWilson. **GIDP:** Duncan.

Runners left in scoring position: Detroit 6 (Granderson 2, Casey, IRodriguez, Polanco, Bonderman); St. Louis 4 (Taguchi, Pujols, Suppan, Rodriguez).

Runners moved up: Polanco 2, PrWilson. **DP:** Detroit 1 (CGuillen and Casey).

Detroit	ip	h	r	er	bb	so	np	era
Bonderman	5⅓	6	2	2	4	4	92	3.38
Rodney BS, 1	1⅓	2	2	0	1	4	30	3.00
Zumaya (L, 0-1)	1	1	1	1	1	1	19	4.50

St. Louis	ip	h	r	er	bb	so	np	era
Suppan	6	8	3	3	2	4	87	4.50
Kinney	⅔	0	0	0	1	1	13	0.00
TJohnson	⅓	0	0	0	0	0	1	0.00
Looper H, 1	⅓	1	1	1	0	0	6	3.86
Wainwright (W, 1-0) (BS, 1)								
	1⅔	1	0	0	3	23	0.00	

Inherited runners-scored: Rodney 2-0, Wainwright 1-1, TJohnson 1-0.
IBB: off Rodney (Pujols) 1, off Bonderman (Miles) 1, off Suppan (Inge) 1. **WP:** Zumaya.
Umpires: Home, Mike Winters; 1b, John Hirschbeck; 2b, Tim McClelland; 3b, Randy Marsh; Left, Alfonso Marquez; Right, Wally Bell.
T: 3:35. **A:** 46,470. (43,975).

JULIAN H. GONZALEZ

SO CLOSE IN THE EIGHTH: Tigers leftfielder Craig Monroe can't quite make the catch of David Eckstein's two-out line drive in the eighth inning. When the ball bounced off Monroe's glove, Aaron Miles scored from second base with the run that broke a 4-4 tie. For Eckstein, who's 5-feet-7 and 165 pounds, it was his fourth hit of the night.

to be 3-1," Jim Leyland said of the Cardinals, after his Tigers dropped a heartbreaker, 5-4, "and we've played good enough to be 1-3."

It will hurt. It will haunt.

"We've done a few things ... to either give them a run or give them some extra chances," Leyland said, "and they're obviously a good enough team to take advantage of those."

Since when did the pitchers on this team suddenly lose the ability to make the simplest throws? Is it nerves? Youth? Something contagious?

Maybe it's all three. In the eighth inning, Joel Zumaya — who struggled in his last outing — threw a wild third strike that Pudge Rodriguez couldn't stop and allowed Aaron Miles to move up to second base. And because he got

FLOODED

The ghost of Curt Flood exacted its revenge 38 years later on another Curtis.

Flood, the Gold Glove St. Louis centerfielder, misjudged Tiger Jim Northrup's drive late in Game 7 of the 1968 World Series. Normally sure-footed, Flood stumbled, and the ball sailed over his head for a Series-decisive two-run triple.

This time it was Curtis Granderson slipping and spinning, perhaps providing the enduring snapshot of a Tigers' World Series disaster.

Playing a shallow center in the bottom of the seventh in Game 4, Granderson thought he'd easily track David Eckstein's fly ball. He pivoted, but instead of sprinting back at top speed, he

hit the wet turf. Granderson frantically scrambled to his feet, but the ball sailed over his head, and Eckstein stood at second with the double.

And then everything fell apart. A team whose signature was late-inning calm in the face of the storm unraveled from the force of a determined St. Louis team that looks undeniable.

"I can't beat myself up over it," Granderson said. "If I do that, I can't focus on what I need to do. We've got another game, and we've got to get ready for it. We've got to put this behind us because it's not over yet. It's the first one to four."

BY DREW SHARP

to second base — a base he never should have had — he was able to score on David Eckstein's double that sealed the victory, that sharp line drive that caromed off the edge of Monroe's glove.

"It's nice," said Eckstein, who looks like a 12-year-old Doogie Howser, "to have a little luck involved."

Leyland had a different take on it. "That's baseball," he said.

Now the Tigers have to win three straight — two of which would be in Comerica Park.

So it's possible (they did it in 1968 vs. these same Cards). But it's not probable. The Tigers blew it on a night when two of their formerly goose-egged hitters came alive, Rodriguez (3-for-4, a double, an RBI, a run scored) and Granderson (1-for-5, a double, a run scored.) But Magglio Ordonez (0-for-5) has lost his hero's halo. And Placido Polanco, the ALCS MVP, is still hitless.

Brink job. This is how it feels, you're out on that edge, looking down at the deep. Earlier in the day, they had said this game would be rained out. But that wasn't true. Because weather changes.

Can fortunes?

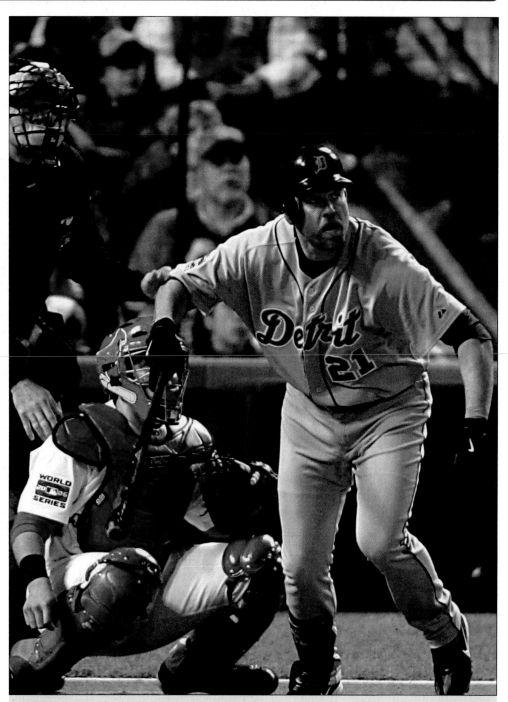

ERIC SEALS

Sean Casey hits a home run in the second inning of Game 4. The Tigers took a 3-0 lead early, and Casey played a role in all three runs.

THE LONE SHINING TIGER

Sean Casey wasn't a Tiger at the start of the season, but he's sure happy he is now.

He became a full-time major leaguer back in 1998, but until this year, he had never tasted the postseason.

And in the World Series, he's shining. Casey went 3-for-4 in Game 4 and is 6-for-13 in this Series.

With a little more help from his friends, Casey would have been the hero in Game 4. Instead, the Tigers fell a little short — maybe one at-bat short. The Tigers' final out came on a Magglio Ordonez groundout. In the on-deck circle, Sean Casey could only watch.

BY MICHAEL ROSENBERG

Oops, they did it again. The Tigers committed error after error in the Series. The Cardinals' Yadier Molina scored after Justin Verlander's errant throw in Game 5.

JULIAN H. GONZALEZ

NO MAGIC LEFT

Leyland can do only so much when hitters fail

By Michael Rosenberg

ST. LOUIS — And in the end, manager Jim Leyland reached into his bag of tricks and found only lint.

There was nothing left to do. No backup outfielders to stick in the line-up so they could hit a home run. No reason to pull his starting pitcher in the middle of an at-bat. No use in yelling; no benefit to cheerleading. The emperor had no options.

The fifth and final game of the 2006 World Series featured more nightmarish moments for the Tigers. Brandon Inge got caught in a rundown after a baserunning mistake. Justin Verlander made a throwing error, the fifth error for a Tigers pitcher in this series.

For the Tigers, who seemed to have an endless supply of magic in their clubhouse, all the little disasters against the Cardinals must have been jarring.

Even with the errors, the Tigers allowed only 22 runs — 4.4 per game. In the regular season, they allowed 4.2.

They scored only 11 runs, and 11 runs in five World Series games are not enough, no matter how fancy your glove work.

His players never stopped believing. They just stopped hitting.

"You think you're going to put a couple of (runs) on the board, get things going, get a big inning," said Sean Casey, the best Tigers hitter in the Series by a mile. "That big inning never just came."

Rarely in Detroit sports history has a coach or manager gotten so much credit for a team's success.

But these players had never seen anything like him.

"Never, never, never, never, never," Casey said. "I've been here three months, and he's the best manager I've ever played for. I'd heard so many great things about him, but he exceeded my expectations."

So many of Leyland's decisions worked that his players just figured that whatever Leyland did would work.

The game began with a controversial Leyland decision — starting Verlander, who seemed gassed, instead of the veteran Rogers.

It was an easy decision to rip, even though nobody knew how Rogers would pitch in St. Louis; and the Tigers needed three wins, not one.

And it worked, too. After a first inning when he looked as nervous as a first-year pitcher — in Little League — Verlander pitched six quality innings.

It just wasn't enough.

One of the most magical Tigers seasons ever ended with a strikeout by Inge, which pretty much summed up this Series.

CHAMPIONSHIP SERIES GAME 5

Cardinals ..4
Tigers 2

COUNTDOWN

Playoff wins Tigers need to win the 2007 World Series.

HERO

JEFF WEAVER
He shut down his former team on four hits for eight innings.

GOAT

JUSTIN VERLANDER
Maybe Kenny Rogers should have started.

TWO CENTS
Wait till next year, eh? You know, even with the way it ended, with this Tigers team we can't wait till next year.

IN PRINT

Third baseman Brandon Inge tries his best to field Justin Verlander's wayward throw. But Inge couldn't snare it, and the Cardinals ended up scoring a run. MANDI WRIGHT

ERIC SEALS

After being crowned MVP of the ALCS, Placido Polanco, who couldn't beat the Cardinals' Jeff Weaver to first in the seventh inning of Game 5, had a dismal Series. He failed to record a hit in 17 at-bats.

THE TIGERS TOP TEN
THINGS WE'LL REMEMBER ABOUT THE 2006 TIGERS

10. Zumaya's arm and fist-pump: They were worth the price of admission.

9. All-Star Game: Ordonez, Rodriguez, Rogers and home field were enough reasons to watch.

8. Chris Shelton's start: Nine homers in his first 13 games.

7. Jim Leyland: He smoked, wore spikes and inspired everyone into believing in this team.

6. Justin Verlander: The majors' top rookie ran out of gas, but just imagine how good he will be for years to come.

5. Late-inning heroics: The Tigers couldn't go a week without gripping drama on the field.

4. The Gambler: Once troubled, he found a home in Detroit.

3. Gum Time: Big League Chew never tasted so good.

2. Champagne showers: The ALDS and ALCS celebrations will go down as where-were-you-when moments.

1. Maggs' blast: Worth every penny of the $75 million.

MANDI WRIGHT

Pudge Rodriguez and Nate Robertson are gracious losers, shaking hands with Cardinals reliever Braden Looper after Game 5. The Cardinals' 85 regular-season wins were the fewest for any World Series winner in a non-shortened season.

QUOTABLES

Compiled from staff reports, news services and MLB.com:

■ Placido Polanco, interviewed on FSN postgame: "I think God will punish us if we're not satisfied with the kind of year that we all had here."

■ Pudge Rodriguez: "We were in the playoffs and in the World Series because we played good defense and we pitched good."

■ Jim Leyland: "The bright side is no one will be complaining about PFP (pitchers' fielding practice) next spring."

■ Rookie Andrew Miller lost in the College World Series before joining the Tigers. He traveled to St. Louis with the team, even though he was not on the playoff roster: "I hope I'm not bad luck."

■ Todd Jones: "There's no bitter end to this story."

■ Sean Casey: "They just flat-out beat us. But you know what? To go from 20 games under .500 and end up in the World Series, that to me is quite an accomplishment."

■ Kenny Rogers: "If anybody says we weren't ready, they forget we were ready for the Yankees, we were ready for the A's. It wasn't about being ready, it was about execution."

■ Jeff Weaver: "I don't think there's a guy in here that wanted to go back to Detroit. We wanted to do it here."

SECOND-GUESSING

Where was Kenny Rogers?
Why didn't he demand the ball from manager Jim Leyland in this situation, considering he had pitched 23 consecutive scoreless innings?
Leyland said that if Game 5 were a Game 7, Rogers would get the call.
Well, this was a Game 7 — the first of three straight win-or-else ultimatums as the Tigers tried for one final, incredible comeback.
Rogers couldn't have performed more scared than Justin Verlander in a 35-pitch scoreless, hitless first inning. Leyland was so panicked he had Jason Grilli up and tossing after Verlander's third batter.

BY DREW SHARP

Amid the cheering Cardinals fans, all Justin Verlander could do was watch as Detroit's title dreams slipped away. MANDI WRIGHT

Rookies' title time will come

Maturity of young Tigers will fortify future championships

By Drew Sharp

ST. LOUIS — The haunting memories will linger in the young Tigers' heads in what now will become a frustrating winter.

And that's not a bad thing.

Justin Verlander remained in the dugout after the final out in Game 5 against the Cardinals — the vanquished observing the victorious.

Hadn't he already endured enough torture?

The impulse after the Tigers' atrocious exhibition of fundamentally poor baseball is to strip the memory of it, crumble it into a ball and toss it into the trash.

But considering their World Series, the Tigers probably would miss the can.

"We cut our own throats," Verlander said afterward in the solemn clubhouse.

The rookies who blossomed beyond all expectation this season shouldn't forget how hard they were humbled at the end. The best education for them is remembering an innocent slip in centerfield or an unconscionable throwing error or an ill-timed wild pitch.

JULIAN H. GONZALEZ

St. Louis relief pitcher Adam Wainwright delivered the final blow with his strikeout of Brandon Inge in the ninth inning of Game 5.

It's too easy to say Verlander, Joel Zumaya and Curtis Granderson choked under the intimidating glare of international spotlight.

And it's not fair.

Detroit grew so spoiled with their flair for the dramatic that it forgot they were rookies.

And rookies get scared, moving too fast too soon.

Their misfortune is what will endure from the Tigers' stunning five-game elimination from the World Series. Granderson's "the Slip" in the seventh inning of

Game 4 — quite possibly the turning point of the Series. Zumaya's awful control and reckless throwing error that scored two runs in Game 3. And Verlander's throwing error — his second of the series — in the fourth inning in Game 5 bringing in the tying run and switching the momentum.

"You can't go through this game of baseball and expect to be on top of the world the whole time," said Granderson. "And none of us have done that. We've had our down spots, and we're learning from them and trying our best to get out of them.

"You learn through adversity. Understand what it takes to get out of those down spots and trying to avoid them in the future."

Maturity isn't rushed. It crawls along at its own pace. But this harsh experience will serve the rookies well if it toughens their hide and emboldens their spirit. A disappointing finish can't diminish the overall impact of baseball's return to relevance in Detroit.

Making the World Series isn't a mirage. "It'll take some time, but we'll take something out of this that will help us," Verlander said. "We're heading in the right direction, and it's our objective to get back here."

TIME CAPSULE: THE YEAR THE TIGERS ROARED

It wasn't all about the Tigers. Some other things that happened on the same year they advanced to their first World Series since 1984:

- The world beat on America in basketball (again) ... in baseball ... in Ryder Cup golf (AGAIN) ... in soccer (it was supposed to be our year!) ... in competitive eating (will no one unseat hot dog-munching Kobayashi?).
- Katie Couric left NBC's "Today" show for the "CBS Evening News."
- Meredith Vieira left "The View" for "Today," and Rosie O'Donnell took her spot at "The View."
- Stevie Y left the ice for the Wings' front office.
- Ben Wallace left for Chicago, spurning the Pistons and their fans for more money.
- Brendan Shanahan left for New York and received hearty thanks and good luck from Red Wings fans.
- The NBA made it illegal for players to whine about officiating — aka the 'Sheed Rule.
- Tom Cruise got dumped by Paramount Pictures for erratic behavior — and his religion, Scientology, took further hits as "South Park" received an Emmy nod for ripping on it — and found a new home with a film company owned by Redskins owner Daniel Snyder.
- Cruise also tried vaguely to apologize to Brooke Shields for publicly criticizing her use of antidepressants.
- Shields' ex-hubby, Andre Agassi, bid a tearful good-bye at the U.S. Open.
- Roger Federer won the U.S. Open and was cheered on by new best buddy Tiger Woods.
- Woods, well, won a lot this year — except in the Ryder Cup.
- No Cup was hoisted in Detroit this year ... except for Detroiter and Compuware founder Peter Karmanos getting a chance to hoist the Stanley Cup after his Carolina Hurricanes won it.
- The South was the place to be in the NBA as well. The Heat rode D-Wade and some officiating (at least according to Dallas owner Mark Cuban) past the Pistons and Mavericks to its first title.
- The Lions did not win their first Super Bowl title in 40 years — despite the chance for a home game at Ford Field.
- But the Shock won its second WNBA title in less than 10 years. Mattawan celebrated an LLWS in softball. Here's to the ladies of Michigan!
- Cinderella George Mason upset Michigan

AMY LEANG

Guard Deanna Nolan, left, and forward Swin Cash celebrate the Shock's second WNBA title. The Shock, led by coach Bill Laimbeer, clinched its victory at Joe Louis Arena, because their regular home, the Palace, hosted a Mariah Carey concert.

RASHAUN RUCKER

Tigers fans showed their pride at Lions games, where the team wasn't so successful. The Lions lost their first five games of 2006.

State — and many others — to advance to the Final Four. But Florida won the title.

- The Wolverines hoopsters proved themselves to be the 67th-best team in the nation with an NIT runner-up finish.
- Lloyd Carr won at Notre Dame. Firelloydcarr.com went on hiatus.
- John L. Smith slapped himself in the face.
- T.O. O.D.'d and so did the media.
- And 2006 will go down as the year Americans whined about gas (but did nothing), watched Howie Mandel resurrect his career ("Deal or No Deal"), worried about potential nukes from North

KIRTHMON F. DOZIER

Coach Lloyd Carr got a Carr wash after the Wolverines beat Notre Dame at South Bend. Michigan remained undefeated throughout the Tigers' postseason run.

JULIAN H. GONZALEZ

Pistons forward Rasheed Wallace defends Miami Heat forward Antoine Walker in the Eastern Conference finals. The Pistons, who had gone to two straight NBA Finals, were eliminated by the Heat.

Korea, gasped over "Grey's Anatomy" and went ga ga over the "Pirates" (no, not Pittsburgh — the Johnny Depp film set in the Caribbean).

BY KYLE O'NEILL

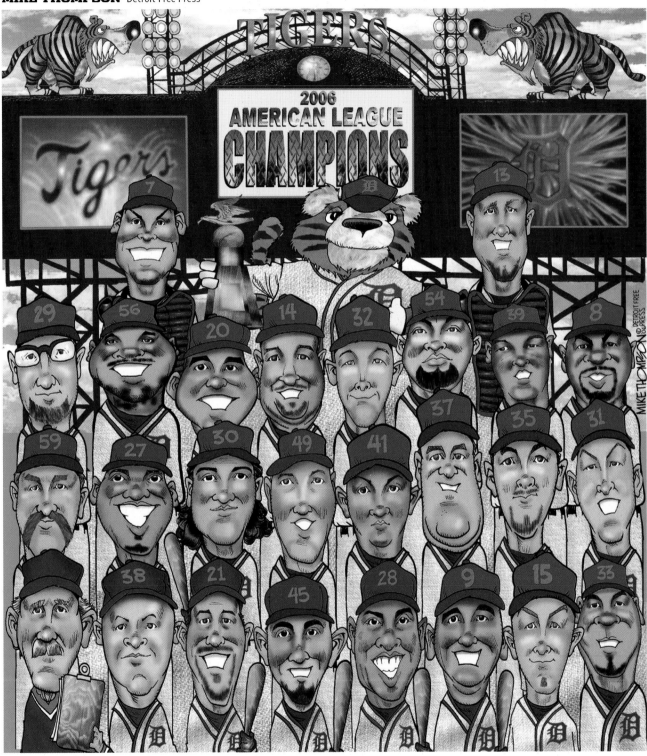

Paws is the official mascot of the Tigers. He doesn't talk, but he has been prowling around games since 1995. Of course, if you want Paws to pay a visit to your event, MLB.com reports his appearance fees start at $125 an hour.

Debbie Kozer of St. Clair Shores attends Bark in the Park with her Westie terrier Levi on June 13. Each owner was asked to take "Doggy Poo Bags" for accidents and sign a waiver. There was a warning at the bottom of the waiver: "Do not bring a female dog in heat."

7 | THE CLOSER

Tigers fans wave towels during Game 4 of the ALDS against the Yankees. PAUL SANCYA/Associated Press

MANDI WRIGHT

Jonathan Rinkinen, 21, of Highland helps clean the clubhouse as Nate Robertson reads a paper before a Tigers game on June 15. Batboys, or more accurately, clubhouse boys, do laundry, help prepare meals and do work on the field. They must be 16 years old, and wages range from $6.50 to $9 per hour, plus tips. For a regular 7 p.m. start, they arrive at noon and stay until about midnight.

KIRTHMON F. DOZIER

Shelby Aggas, left, and her sister, Alyssa, 11, of Warren receive an autograph from Vance Wilson. Almost 2.6 million fans came to Comerica Park to explore its carousel, Ferris wheel, centerfield fountain and sculptures of Ty Cobb, Willie Horton and other Tigers greats.

Jeff Daniels performs his song, "The Lifelong Tiger Fan Blues Revisited," at a Tigers rally before the playoffs. He sings: "All my hopes and dreams all in place. I get visions of my Tigers in a pennant race."

RASHAUN RUCKER

AMY LEANG

Tigers fans Danielle Cossick, left, 23, of Howell and Kimberly Dwyer, 25, of Brighton go for a spin on the carousel Aug. 24. The festive atmosphere at Comerica Park is fueled by loud rock and Latino music and lots of 20- and 30-something fans.

Mario Impemba, left, and Rod Allen call Tigers games for FSN. "Watching (Justin) Verlander, watching (Joel) Zumaya, watching all the pieces come together. I had a feeling at the beginning of the year that they had a chance to contend in the Central," Allen said. The ex-Tiger (he played briefly on the 1984 team) became a fan-favorite. DAVID P. GILKEY

TIGERS' REGULAR SEASON

= WIN

APRIL	OPPONENT	RESULT	REC	WIN	LOSS
3	at KC	W 3-1	1-0	Rogers (1-0)	Elarton (0-1)
5	at KC	W 14-3	2-0	Bonderman (1-0)	Mays (0-1)
6	at Tex.	W 10-6	3-0	Robertson (1-0)	Dickey (0-1)
7	at Tex.	W 5-2	4-0	Maroth (1-0)	Koronka (0-1)
8	at Tex.	W 7-0	5-0	Verlander (1-0)	Millwood (0-2)
Sun. 9	at Tex.	L 5-3	5-1	Padilla (2-0)	Rogers (1-1)
10	CWS	L 5-3	5-2	Garcia (1-1)	Bonderman (1-1)
12	CWS	L 4-3	5-3	Contreras (1-0)	Robertson (1-1)
13	CWS	L 13-9	5-4	Garland (1-1)	Verlander (1-1)
14	Cle.	W 5-1	6-4	Rogers (2-1)	Westbrook (2-1)
15	Cle.	L 7-2	6-5	Carmona (1-0)	Bonderman (1-2)
Sun. 16	Cle.	W 1-0	7-5	Maroth (2-0)	Lee (1-1)
17	Cle.	L 10-2	7-6	Byrd (2-1)	Robertson (1-2)
18	at Oak.	L 4-3	7-7	Duchscherer (1-0)	Verlander (1-2)
19	at Oak.	W 11-4	8-7	Rogers (3-1)	Blanton (1-2)
20	at Oak.	W 4-3	9-7	Rodney (1-0)	Duchscherer (1-1)
21	at Sea.	W 2-1	10-7	Maroth (3-0)	Washburn (1-3)
22	at Sea.	W 2-0	11-7	Robertson (2-2)	Meche (1-1)
Sun. 23	at Sea.	W 6-4	12-7	Verlander (2-2)	Hernandez (0-3)
24	at LAA	L 3-0	12-8	Santana (2-0)	Rogers (3-2)
25	at LAA	W 5-2	13-8	Bonderman (2-2)	Carrasco (0-1)
26	at LAA	L 4-0	13-9	Lackey (3-1)	Maroth (3-1)
28	Min.	W 9-0	14-9	Robertson (3-2)	Radke (2-3)
29	Min.	W 18-1	15-9	Verlander (3-2)	Silva (1-4)
Sun. 30	Min.	W 6-0	16-9	Rogers (4-2)	Lohse (1-2)

MAY	OPPONENT	RESULT	REC	WIN	LOSS
1	KC	W 3-2	17-9	Bonderman (3-2)	Hernandez (1-1)
2	KC	W 4-1	18-9	Maroth (4-1)	Redman (0-2)
3	LAA	W 2-1	19-9	Zumaya (1-0)	Weaver (0-1)
4	LAA	L 7-2	19-10	Gregg (2-0)	Verlander (3-3)
5	at Min.	W 9-6	20-10	Rogers (5-2)	Lohse (1-3)
6	at Min.	L 7-6	20-11	Rincon (2-0)	Jones (0-1)
Sun. 7	at Min.	L 4-2	20-12	Santana (3-3)	Maroth (4-2)
9	at Bal.	L 7-6	20-13	Hawkins (1-1)	Rodney (1-1)
10	at Bal.	W 6-3	21-13	Verlander (4-3)	Lopez (1-5)
11	at Bal.	Postponed	N/A		
12	at Cle.	W 5-4	22-13	Rogers (6-2)	Lee (2-4)
13	at Cle.	W 3-0	23-13	Bonderman (4-2)	Sabathia (2-3)
Sun. 14	at Cle.	W 3-2	24-13	Maroth (5-2)	Johnson (2-3)
16	Min.	W 7-4	25-13	Robertson (4-2)	Lohse (2-4)
17	Min.	W 2-0	26-13	Verlander (5-3)	Santana (4-4)
18	Min.	W 5-3	27-13	Rogers (7-2)	Radke (4-5)
19	Cin.	L 9-4	27-14	Claussen (3-4)	Bonderman (4-3)
20	Cin.	W 7-6	28-14	Rodney (2-1)	Weathers (1-2)
Sun. 21	Cin.	W 1-0	29-14	Rodney (3-1)	Harang (5-3)
22	at KC	W 8-0	30-14	Verlander (6-3)	Affeldt (2-4)
23	at KC	W 8-5	31-14	Zumaya (2-0)	Dessens (2-4)
24	at KC	W 6-3	32-14	Bonderman (5-3)	Gobble (0-1)
25	at KC	W 13-8	33-14	Zumaya (3-0)	Dessens (2-5)
26	Cle.	W 8-3	34-14	Robertson (5-2)	Westbrook (4-3)
27	Cle.	W 3-1	35-14	Verlander (7-3)	Byrd (4-4)
Sun. 28	Cle.	L 9-0	35-15	Johnson (3-4)	Rogers (7-3)
29	NYY	L 4-0	35-16	Johnson (7-4)	Bonderman (5-4)
30	NYY	L 11-6	35-17	Rivera (3-3)	Jones (0-2)
31	NYY	L 6-1	35-18	Mussina (7-1)	Robertson (5-3)

JUNE	OPPONENT	RESULT	REC	WIN	LOSS
1	NYY	W 7-6	36-18	Rodney (4-1)	Farnsworth (1-3)
2	Bos.	L 3-2	36-19	Seanez (1-0)	Jones (0-3)
3	Bos.	W 6-2	37-19	Bonderman (6-4)	Wakefield (4-7)
Sun. 4	Bos.	L 8-3	37-20	Clement (5-4)	Miner (0-1)
6	at CWS	L 4-3	37-21	McCarthy (3-3)	Rodney (4-2)
7	at CWS	L 4-3	37-22	Contreras (6-0)	Verlander (7-4)
8	at CWS	W 6-2	38-22	Rogers (8-3)	Garland (4-3)
9	at Tor.	L 10-5	38-23	Frasor (2-1)	Jones (0-4)
10	at Tor.	W 5-3	39-23	Miner (1-1)	Lilly (5-7)
Sun. 11	at Tor.	W 10-5	40-23	Robertson (6-3)	Taubenheim (0-3)
12	TB	W 4-3	41-23	Jones (1-4)	Meadows (1-1)
13	TB	W 7-1	42-23	Rogers (9-3)	McClung (2-9)
14	TB	L 5-1	42-24	Meadows (2-1)	Jones (1-5)
15	TB	W 6-2	43-24	Miner (2-1)	Fossum (2-3)
16	at CHC	W 5-3	44-24	Robertson (7-3)	Rusch (2-7)
17	at CHC	W 9-3	45-24	Verlander (8-4)	Marmol (1-1)
Sun. 18	at CHC	W 12-3	46-24	Rogers (10-3)	Prior (0-1)
19	at Mil.	W 3-1	47-24	Bonderman (7-4)	Wise (4-4)
20	at Mil.	W 10-1	48-24	Miner (3-1)	Helling (0-3)
21	at Mil.	L 4-3	48-25	Capuano (8-4)	Zumaya (3-1)
23	StL	W 10-6	49-25	Verlander (9-4)	Carpenter (6-4)
24	StL	W 7-6	50-25	Zumaya (4-1)	Johnson (3-4)
Sun. 25	StL	W 4-1	51-25	Ledezma (1-0)	Ponson (4-3)
26	Hou.	W 10-4	52-25	Miner (4-1)	Rodriguez (8-5)
27	Hou.	W 4-0	53-25	Robertson (8-3)	Clemens (1-1)
28	Hou.	W 5-0	54-25	Verlander (10-4)	Pettitte (6-9)
30	at Pit.	W 7-6	55-25	Colon (1-0)	Wells (0-3)

JULY	OPPONENT	RESULT	REC	WIN	LOSS
1	at Pit.	L 9-2	55-26	Capps (3-1)	Grilli (0-1)
Sun. 2	Pit.	W 9-8	56-26	Miner (5-1)	Snell (7-6)
3	at Oak.	L 5-3	56-27	Blanton (8-7)	Robertson (8-4)
4	at Oak.	L 2-1	56-28	Gaudin (1-2)	Rodney (4-3)
5	at Oak.	W 10-4	57-28	Rogers (11-3)	Saarloos (0-1)
7	at Sea.	W 6-1	58-28	Bonderman (8-4)	Pineiro (6-8)
8	at Sea.	W 2-1	59-28	Miner (6-1)	Washburn (4-9)
Sun. 9	at Sea.	L 3-2	59-29	Meche (8-4)	Robertson (8-5)
13	KC	W 6-4	60-29	Bonderman (9-4)	Duckworth (1-2)
14	KC	W 10-9	61-29	Jones (2-5)	Affeldt (4-6)
15	KC	W 6-0	62-29	Verlander (11-4)	Gobble (3-3)
Sun. 16	KC	L 9-6	62-30	Elarton (4-9)	Miner (6-2)
18	CWS	L 7-1	62-31	Garland (9-3)	Robertson (8-6)
19	CWS	W 5-2	63-31	Bonderman (10-4)	Vazquez (9-5)
20	CWS	W 2-1	64-31	Zumaya (5-1)	Contreras (9-2)
21	Oak.	W 7-4	65-31	Verlander (12-4)	Haren (6-9)
22	Oak.	L 9-5	65-32	Blanton (10-8)	Ledezma (1-1)
Sun. 23	Oak.	W 8-4	66-32	Robertson (9-6)	Loaiza (4-6)
24	at Cle.	W 9-7	67-32	Bonderman (11-4)	Lee (9-8)
25	at Cle.	L 12-7	67-33	Davis (3-1)	Rogers (11-4)
26	at Cle.	W 4-1	68-33	Verlander (13-4)	Sabathia (7-7)
28	at Min.	W 3-2	69-33	Rodney (5-3)	Rincon (3-1)
29	at Min.	W 8-6	70-33	Robertson (10-6)	Radke (9-8)
Sun. 30	at Min.	L 6-4	70-34	Neshek (1-0)	Bonderman (11-5)
31	at TB	L 7-3	70-35	Fossum (5-4)	Rogers (11-5)

AUG.	OPPONENT	RESULT	REC	WIN	LOSS
1	at TB	W 10-4	71-35	Verlander (14-4)	Howell (0-1)
2	at TB	W 8-3	72-35	Grilli (1-1)	Switzer (2-2)
3	at TB	L 2-1	72-36	McClung (3-10)	Robertson (10-7)
4	Cle.	W 7-6	73-36	Colon (2-0)	Cabrera (1-2)
5	Cle.	W 4-3	74-36	Zumaya (6-1)	Carmona (1-7)
Sun. 6	Cle.	W 1-0	75-36	Ledezma (2-1)	Sabathia (8-8)
7	Min.	W 9-3	76-36	Miner (7-2)	Liriano (12-3)
8	Min.	L 4-2	76-37	Radke (11-8)	Robertson (10-8)
9	Min.	L 8-3	76-38	Santana (13-5)	Zumaya (6-2)
11	at CWS	L 5-0	76-39	Contreras (11-4)	Verlander (14-5)
12	at CWS	L 4-3	76-40	MacDougal (1-0)	Rogers (11-6)
Sun. 13	at CWS	L 7-3	76-41	Garcia (11-7)	Miner (7-3)
14	at Bos.	W 7-4	77-41	Robertson (11-8)	Beckett (13-7)
15	at Bos.	W 3-2	78-41	Rodney (6-3)	Timlin (5-2)
16	at Bos.	L 6-4	78-42	Wells (2-2)	Verlander (14-6)
17	Tex.	W 4-2	79-42	Rogers (12-6)	Volquez (1-1)
18	Tex.	L 2-1	79-43	Millwood (12-8)	Miner (7-4)
19	Tex.	L 3-1	79-44	Tejeda (2-3)	Robertson (11-9)
Sun. 20	Tex.	L 7-6	79-45	Benoit (1-1)	Grilli (1-2)
21	CWS	W 7-1	80-45	Verlander (15-6)	Contreras (11-6)
22	CWS	W 4-0	81-45	Rogers (13-6)	Buehrle (10-11)
23	CWS	L 7-5	81-46	Garcia (12-8)	Miner (7-5)
24	CWS	L 10-0	81-47	Garland (15-4)	Robertson (11-10)
25	at Cle.	L 4-2	81-48	Sowers (6-3)	Bonderman (11-6)
26	at Cle.	L 8-5	81-49	Westbrook (11-8)	Verlander (15-7)
Sun. 27	at Cle.	W 7-1	82-49	Rogers (14-6)	Lee (10-10)
29	at NYY	Postponed	N/A		
30	at NYY	L 2-0	82-50	Wang (16-5)	Robertson (11-11)
30	at NYY	W 5-3	83-50	Grilli (2-2)	Proctor (5-4)
31	at NYY	L 6-4	83-51	Johnson (15-10)	Bonderman (11-7)

SEPT.	OPPONENT	RESULT	REC	WIN	LOSS
1	LAA	W 9-0	84-51	Rogers (15-6)	Santana (13-7)
2	LAA	L 7-2	84-52	Rodriguez (2-2)	Jones (2-6)
Sun. 3	LAA	L 2-1	84-53	Escobar (10-12)	Ledezma (2-2)
4	Sea.	W 6-2	85-53	Robertson (12-11)	Washburn (8-13)
5	Sea.	L 4-3	85-54	Pineiro (8-11)	Miller (0-1)
6	Sea.	L 5-4	85-55	Huber (1-0)	Zumaya (6-3)
7	at Min.	W 7-2	86-55	Verlander (16-7)	Baker (4-8)
8	at Min.	L 9-5	86-56	Neshek (4-1)	Ledezma (2-3)
9	at Min.	L 2-1	86-57	Bonser (5-5)	Robertson (12-12)
Sun. 10	at Min.	L 12-1	86-58	Santana (18-5)	Bonderman (11-8)
12	Tex.	W 3-2	87-58	Rodney (7-3)	Mahay (1-3)
13	Tex.	L 11-3	87-59	Millwood (15-10)	Verlander (16-8)
15	Bal.	W 17-2	88-59	Bonderman (12-8)	Penn (0-3)
16	Bal.	W 2-0	89-59	Robertson (13-12)	Benson (10-11)
Sun. 17	Bal.	L 12-8	89-60	Ray (3-4)	Grilli (2-3)
18	at CWS	W 8-2	90-60	Rogers (16-6)	Buehrle (12-13)
19	at CWS	L 7-0	90-61	Garcia (15-9)	Verlander (16-9)
20	at CWS	W 6-2	91-61	Bonderman (13-8)	Garland (18-7)
21	at Bal.	L 4-3	91-62	Benson (11-11)	Rodney (7-4)
22	at KC	W 7-3	92-62	Ledezma (3-3)	Hudson (7-6)
23	at KC	W 15-4	93-62	Rogers (17-6)	Redman (10-10)
Sun. 24	at KC	W 11-4	94-62	Verlander (17-9)	Hernandez (6-10)
26	Tor.	W 4-3	95-62	Bonderman (14-8)	McGowan (1-2)
27	Tor.	L 7-4	95-63	Lilly (15-13)	Robertson (13-13)
28	Tor.	L 8-6	95-64	Burnett (10-8)	Rogers (17-7)
29	KC	L 9-7	95-65	Greinke (1-0)	Walker (0-1)
30	KC	L 9-6	95-66	Wellemeyer (1-2)	Miner (7-6)

OCT.	OPPONENT	RESULT	REC	WIN	LOSS
Sun. 1	KC	L 10-8	95-67	Gobble (4-6)	Rogers (17-8)

Brandon Inge hit .253 with 27 homers and 83 RBIs in the regular season. He also improved his defensive play at third base. His World Series highlight came in Game 2 against the Cardinals when he had two hits.

TIGERS STATISTICS, 2006

BATTING

NAME	g	ab	r	h	2b	3b	hr	rbi	bb	so	sb	ba	obp	slg	ops
Carlos Guillen	153	543	100	174	41	5	19	85	71	87	20	.320	.400	.519	.920
Ivan Rodriguez	136	547	74	164	28	4	13	69	26	86	8	.300	.332	.437	.769
Magglio Ordonez	155	593	82	177	32	1	24	104	45	87	1	.298	.350	.477	.827
Placido Polanco	110	461	58	136	18	1	4	52	17	27	1	.295	.329	.364	.693
Vance Wilson	56	152	18	43	9	0	5	18	2	33	0	.283	.304	.441	.745
Brent Clevlen	31	39	9	11	1	2	3	6	2	15	0	.282	.317	.641	.958
Omar Infante	78	224	35	62	11	4	4	25	14	45	3	.277	.325	.415	.740
Chris Shelton	115	373	50	102	16	4	16	47	34	107	1	.273	.340	.466	.806
Alexis Gomez	62	103	17	28	5	2	1	6	6	21	4	.272	.318	.388	.707
Curtis Granderson	159	596	90	155	31	9	19	68	66	174	8	.260	.335	.438	.773
Marcus Thames	110	348	61	89	20	2	26	60	37	92	1	.256	.333	.549	.882
Craig Monroe	147	541	89	138	35	2	28	92	37	126	2	.255	.301	.482	.783
Brandon Inge	159	542	83	137	29	2	27	83	43	128	7	.253	.313	.463	.776
Dmitri Young	48	172	19	43	4	1	7	23	11	39	1	.250	.293	.407	.700
Sean Casey	53	184	17	45	7	0	5	30	10	21	0	.245	.286	.364	.650
Matt Stairs	14	41	5	10	3	0	2	8	3	12	0	.244	.295	.463	.759
Ramon Santiago	43	80	9	18	1	1	0	3	1	14	2	.225	.244	.263	.506
Neifi Perez	21	65	4	13	1	0	0	5	3	4	1	.200	.235	.215	.451
TIGERS	162	5,642	822	1,548	294	40	203	785	430	1,133	60	.274	.329	.449	.777
OPPONENTS	162	5,535	675	1,420	263	38	160	642	489	1,003	49	.257	.321	.405	.725

PITCHING

NAME	g	gs	w	l	sv	ip	h	er	r	hr	bb	so	era
Chad Durbin	3	0	0	0	0	6	6	1	1	1	0	3	1.50
Joel Zumaya	62	0	6	3	1	83$\frac{1}{3}$	56	18	20	6	42	97	1.94
Jamie Walker	56	0	0	1	0	48	47	15	15	8	8	37	2.81
Colby Lewis	2	0	0	0	0	3	8	1	1	1	1	5	3.00
Chris Spurling	9	0	0	0	0	11$\frac{1}{3}$	13	4	4	2	4	4	3.18
Fernando Rodney	63	0	7	4	7	71$\frac{1}{3}$	51	28	36	6	34	65	3.52
Wilfredo Ledezma	24	7	3	3	0	60$\frac{1}{3}$	60	24	28	5	23	39	3.58
Justin Verlander	30	30	17	9	0	186	187	75	78	21	60	124	3.63
Kenny Rogers	34	33	17	8	0	204	195	87	97	23	62	99	3.84
Nate Robertson	32	32	13	13	0	208$\frac{2}{3}$	206	89	98	29	67	137	3.84
Todd Jones	62	0	2	6	37	64	70	28	31	4	11	28	3.94
Jeremy Bonderman	34	34	14	8	0	214	214	97	104	18	64	202	4.08
Mike Maroth	13	9	5	2	0	53$\frac{2}{3}$	64	25	26	11	16	24	4.19
Jason Grilli	51	0	2	3	0	62	61	29	31	6	25	31	4.21
Zach Miner	27	16	7	6	0	93	100	50	53	11	32	59	4.84
Roman Colon	20	1	2	0	1	38$\frac{2}{3}$	46	21	21	6	14	25	4.89
Andrew Miller	8	0	0	1	0	10$\frac{1}{3}$	8	7	9	0	10	6	6.10
Jordan Tata	8	0	0	0	0	14$\frac{2}{3}$	14	10	11	1	7	6	6.14
Bobby Seay	14	0	0	0	0	15$\frac{1}{3}$	14	11	11	1	9	12	6.46
TOTALS	162	162	95	67	46	1,448	1,420	618	675	160	489	1,003	3.84

Kenny Rogers was solid in the regular season. He was masterful in the playoffs. But he never got to pitch after Game 2 of the World Series.

ON PAGE 128: Photo mosaic compiled from staff file photos and Tigers fans' photos.
DIANE WEISS, BRIAN TODD, STEVE DORSEY and DAVID PIERCE.